DEBRETT'S
GUIDE TO TRACING YOUR FAMILY TREE

Other Debrett's titles from Headline

Debrett's Correct Form
Debrett's New Guide to Etiquette and
Modern Manners: John Morgan
Debrett's Wedding Guide: Jacqueline Llewelyn-Bowen
Debrett's Guide to Your House: Noel Currer-Briggs
Debrett's Guide to Entertaining: Charles Mosley
Debrett's Guide to Bereavement: Charles Mosley

Debrett's

GUIDE TO TRACING YOUR FAMILY TREE

Noel Currer-Briggs and Royston Gambier

Foreword by Iain Swinnerton

HEADLINE

First published in 1982
by Webb & Bower (Publishers) Ltd

This revised edition first published in 1999
by HEADLINE BOOK PUBLISHING

10 9 8 7 6 5 4 3 2 1

British Library Cataloguing in Publication Data

Currer-Briggs, Noel
   Debrett's guide to tracing your family tree
   1.Genealogy
   I.Title II.Gambier, Royston
   III.Tracing your family tree
   929.1

ISBN 0 7472 2331 9

Typeset by
Letterpart Limited, Reigate, Surrey

Printed and bound in Great Britain by
Mackays of Chatham PLC, Chatham, Kent

HEADLINE BOOK PUBLISHING
A division of Hodder Headline PLC
338 Euston Road
London NW1 3BH

CONTENTS

FOREWORD

❖

IAIN SWINNERTON

President of the Federation of the Family History Societies 1974-97

Genealogy as a science began in the sixteenth century and although the latter part of the nineteenth century saw the establishment of many of our present-day historical and antiquarian societies in which there was great interest in tracing and recording pedigrees, it was mainly carried out by the wealthier members of society – the aristocracy and landowning classes and the business and professional men. I suppose no one ever thought the lower classes also had pedigrees. Certainly, they obviously saw no need for anything as mundane as a society for pedigree-tracers and it was not until 1911 that the first such organization was founded. It is significant that this was called the Society of Genealogists *of London*; it was three years before it was acknowledged that interest was not confined to the capital and the territorial appellation dropped. A study of its early journals shows that the emphasis was still on royal, noble and armigerous families and this persisted for many years.

Nothing else happened on the genealogical scene for over fifty years until Dr S.W. Kingsley-Norris, a Birmingham eye surgeon and genealogical and heraldic enthusiast, decided to form a society to cover the Midland counties and so the Birmingham and Midland Society for Genealogy and Heraldry, the first in the provinces, was founded in 1963. Manchester followed suit in 1964 and over the next ten years similar societies were formed in Cheshire, Hampshire, Kent, Norfolk, Nottingham, Rossendale, Sussex and Yorkshire.

By the early 1970s, several of these were in fairly regular contact with each other and tentative links had been forged with the Society of Genealogists and the Heraldry Society. Then, at a meeting in Birmingham in June 1973, called to enlist support to bring the International Congress on Heraldry and Genealogy to this country, a quite separate resolution to found a British Federation of Genealogical, Heraldic and Allied Societies was adopted with eleven societies enrolling as founder members. This was the turning point and the dawn of the new age of the genealogy of the common man.

They were joined fairly soon, albeit somewhat reluctantly, by the Society of Genealogists and the Heraldry Society. The new Federation set out to found a society in every county in England and was helped by such television programmes as Alex Haley's 'Roots' (subsequently proved to be part fiction) and Gordon Honeycombe's search for his ancestors. Influenced by these, more and more people took up the hobby and societies sprang up all over the United Kingdom. Overseas societies (for obvious reasons mainly in the former colonies) asked to join and by the early 1980s there was a well-established network of societies throughout the English-speaking world. Today the Federation of Family History Societies has 213 member societies in ten countries.

Wherever I go I am asked the same question – why have so many people suddenly taken up this pastime of tracing their ancestors and why are people so keen today on digging up the past? This applies not only to family history – historical and archaeological societies have experienced a similar growth.

I think there are several answers. Undoubtedly, sadly, there are still a few who do it for snobbish reasons in the hope that they will trace a descent from a royal or titled family or simply to be able to boast how far back they can go. Given the English system of primogeniture with younger sons having to go into (or marry) trade and some of our former sovereigns' penchants for extra-marital activities, the first is comparatively easy for many while the second is merely boring. One of the best things that has happened over the last two decades is that genealogy, the tracing of pedigrees, has been largely replaced by the study of family history. Most people now realize that researching their ancestors' occupations, hobbies and politics, as well as their virtues and vices, is so much more interesting and satisfying than merely seeing how far they can trace them back.

I would imagine most people start out of curiosity: a desire to know what sort of people their ancestors were and from whence they came. 'Total ancestry', the study of all one's ancestors, is another good thing that has come out of this new wave of interest; most people now appreciate that we inherit our physical and mental characteristics from both our paternal and maternal progenitors and only our surname from our father's line. Indeed, it is unwise to rely entirely on the paternal name for our descent – as the French have it, *'La mère seulement connait le nom du père!'*

Despite this, the last twenty years have seen the birth of another quite different sort of family history society – the One-Name Society. In these, the members trace all the persons of that surname whether they are related or not. Obviously, most of these are the more unusual surnames – one would not attempt it for Smith or Jones.

I also believe that there are a large number who have taken up tracing their ancestors in a subconcious search for security. We live in a very unstable world and have become a highly mobile race, the advent of the motor car has brought freedom to travel in search of a better environment in which to live, work and educate our children. When I ask my average audience how many were born and brought up in the town or village in which they are now living, the usual answer is only about 10 per cent. The rest are strangers and we all know how the English feel about incomers. A feeling of insecurity about their place in the community can persist for some time and inevitably sets them thinking about the place from which they came and whether the family had always lived there. Experience teaches us that this is not usually the case, our ancestors were far more mobile than we like to think.

I am also asked, 'Should I join a Family History Society?' Over 150,000 people in this country alone have done so but there are many more who are still doing their own thing. The advantages of joining are many, the obvious ones being that you get a chance to meet others with the same interests and problems, and to hear speakers who are experts in different aspects of research as well as people like yourself recounting how they did it. In addition, you have access to the society's publications and genealogical aids, such as the indexes that most societies produce. Who knows, you may even meet someone researching the same family.

Whether you do or don't, this book will help you with one of the most fascinating and enjoyable hobbies there is.

This book, now in its third edition, was first published in 1981 and the fact that yet another edition is now being published merely goes to show the continuing popularity of its subject. When it first appeared, everyone was still using pencil and paper, card indexes and consulting original records whereas most sources are now in microform and can be viewed by fiche and film readers or computers from which photocopies or printouts can be obtained obviating many, many hours of laborious hand-copying of records. The hobby now has several glossy magazines devoted to the subject with feature writers who have a wealth of expertise to share with their readers.

However, there is still nothing quite like doing it yourself and perhaps having the thrill of seeing your long-ago ancestor's signature on a document!

1

FAMILY HISTORY YESTERDAY AND TODAY

◆

Not for many centuries has the family as an institution been under such heavy and sustained attack as it is today, and nowhere is loneliness and the sense of rootlessness more complete than in modern cities. Twentieth-century urban civilization threatens family life in much the same way that traditional Roman values and family traditions were destroyed during the early years of the Empire. Since Western European civilization owes as much to Rome, and especially to Roman ideals of family life, as to the Jews, we should perhaps begin by examining the role of the family in these two cultures.

The religion of ancient Rome was first and foremost the religion of the family. The very word religion means binding together. By extension, this religion of the family became the religion of the state. The central concept of Roman religion was the idea of genius, which begins from the paterfamilias who, in begetting children, becomes the head of a family. His essential character was isolated and given a separate spirit-existence; he carried on the family which owed to him its continuity and looked to him for protection. Thus, as a link in that mysterious chain of father-son-father-son, each individual gained new significance, setting him against a background which, instead of being a continuous surface, was broken up in such a way that one of its pieces became himself. His genius, therefore, was that which placed him in a special relationship to his long-dead forebears and to those of his progeny as yet unborn. Genius was thought of as a chain of mysterious power, linking the family from one generation to another; and it was because of this that the Roman father could see himself as a link in this unseen chain.

The traditional function of the family in Jewish culture was to propagate the race, and the family itself was a close-knit one in which the home was – and still to a large extent is – regarded as the basic religious institution, in which the individual found the completion not only of his personality, but also of his highest personal fulfilment in marriage and the continuation of the larger family. Whereas in Roman society the veneration of one's ancestors was due on account of the example they had set and so was of paramount importance, in Jewish society, especially of the Diaspora, children were the chief concern of their parents, because through them the hope of Jewish survival in a hostile world could be kept alive.

Greek attitudes to family life and to marriage differed markedly from Roman and Jewish attitudes. In Classical times neither married nor unmarried women were regarded as legally entitled to act independently. They remained subject all their lives to the authority of a male citizen, usually their father or husband, but in the absence of either, to a male tutor or near relative. In Periclean Athens women who had been born free had no more political or legal rights than slaves. Their position contrasted strikingly with that of women under the Minoan and Achaean civilizations, who although not considered the equals of men did enjoy much more liberty than they would have been allowed at Athens. Such was the threat of misogyny in ancient Greece that strict laws were passed against celibacy. At Athens, while not prohibited officially, celibacy was, nonetheless, uncongenial to the custom of the country. The desire to have at least one son led most young men to marry sooner or later, though marriage, more often than not, was for convenience or for the promotion of business interests. In fifth-century Athens, at least, wives hardly ever saw their husbands, except in bed. The couple rarely ate together, unless a family reunion took place; children were educated outside the home, the boys in the gymnasia and the girls in the gynecea. Christianity rejected most of what it found in Greek family life, but blended the Roman reverence for ancestral custom and standards of public duty with the Jewish concept of the family, wherein God was seen as the Father of all mankind. To show His love for His earthly children, God had sent His Son to teach that all men were brothers and members of one family, the Church. By the nineteenth century it would be hard to say which element was the more dominant.

There are few who lack all curiosity about their forefathers and nowhere is this truer than among those who have been adopted or brought up without any knowledge of their parentage. It is the natural human instinct to speculate upon one's ancestors – where they lived and what they did – and it is not surprising that ancestral records and genealogies can be found in the earliest records of civilized man. The application of genealogical techniques to the study of genetics and hereditary characteristics from diseases to handwriting will be considered elsewhere, and this application is increasing as the efficiency of method and of diagnosis improves. The actuarial evaluation of risks in the insurance industry, accident proneness, health potential, longevity and even criminal and anti-social tendencies all appear to be inherited either genetically, or because of family, economic and environmental considerations; the study of all these can be enriched by family history, for while much of human behaviour is governed by environment, heredity plays an equal, if not more important, part.

The study of family history is relevant to the laws governing inheritance and intestacy. Peculiarities of custom for succession at various times and in various countries require accurate knowledge of a family if the correct descent is to be legally established. Lawyers, therefore, have need of the skill of genealogists in such circumstances.

Sociology, economics, the study of population movement,

demography and the compatibility of groups of different ethnic origin, likewise depend upon it. For example, a study of the effect upon Kentish coalmining families of the immigration of miners from Durham and Wales early in the present century showed that there was considerable friction due to differences in local customs, speech, culture and behaviour. Although there was integration by marriage, such marriages were never secure, and the consequently disrupted families may well have been a direct cause of a very high rate of delinquency found among their children.

The threat to Jewish family life in the United States and Western Europe is somewhat different from that which faces Christians. In his study of Jewish family life in the United States, Judson T. Landis found that the percentages of divorced and separated parents were 3.3 per cent for the Jews, 7.7 per cent for Roman Catholics and 10 per cent for Protestants, and for those of no religious faith it was 18.2 per cent. But while until recently Jewish families were more closely knit than those of other faiths or none, and probably still are, nevertheless, in recent years the rate of intermarriage between Jews and Gentiles has greatly increased. This tendency, while it must be welcomed on one level as a sign that the Jewish minority is becoming assimilated into the majority culture, at the same time poses a threat to the traditional Jewish family values and, should persecution return, to the ability of the Jewish way of life to survive. In 1963 Erich Rosenthal published a study of intermarriage in the Washington DC area in the *American Jewish Year Book*, which showed that while the overall ratio of Jewish intermarriage was reasonably small, the actual rate among the younger generation, namely those actually marrying at the time, was very much higher. Intermarriage has since become a burning topic for American Jewry, but there is unanimous agreement that intermarriage is growing, will continue to grow, and represents a great danger to the future of the Jewish community.

Genealogy has only recently emerged from a period of unscientific abuse during which it pandered to the conceit of those who indulged in it. Unless the truth is precisely sought and revealed, genealogies are no better than myths or fairy-tales.

The science of genealogy must therefore be based on object-
ively established foundations using rational methods and mature
criteria of proof. Great as his achievement was in tracing his
ancestry to West Africa, this is where Alex Haley, the author of
Roots finally fails. The work of historical demographers, especially of men like Laslett and Wrigley in England or Ganiage and
Goubert in France, has shown scientifically how the classes in
Western European society are constantly changing and that these
changes are no new phenomenon of the twentieth-century
reformers nor the result of a particular economic or social
dogma. This is not to deny the existence of tensions between
groups of people with different social and economic interests and
backgrounds, which are both inevitable and desirable for progress.
The concept of the class struggle and the perpetuation of the
myth that people with a certain background or education behave
in a certain exclusive and anti-social manner against the interests
of the working class (whatever that term may mean) are good
examples of pseudo-scientific half-truths. Both notions are based
on premises which are largely untrue and almost totally illusory.
Historians and sociologists have, to be sure, written about the rise
of the middle classes and the decline of the aristocracy and so
on, but what in fact they have done is to draw general conclu-
sions from a few examples of individuals and their families who
had the ability to influence national and international events, and
who experienced economic success or failure on an exceptional
scale. The power and affluence of the Cecils, Rothschilds or
Wedgwoods were only marginally shared by the whole social class
to which they belonged. Their success (or failure) was due to the
ability and intelligence of a few individuals. If by assortative
mating these families were able to retain their power and
affluence for several generations, this was because the social
conditions in which they lived enabled them to do so. If, however,
we go back to before the Reformation, we find just as many or
just as few examples of men of humble origin attaining great
power and wealth: Wolsey and Becket to name but two. Had it
not been for the Church's rule of celibacy, no doubt they too
would have founded influential families.

THE NEED FOR FAMILY HISTORY

The need for genealogy arose from people's curiosity about their origins. For a long time legends were enough, but genealogy is the purest form of history as it concerns individuals, and, eventually, the desire to find the objective truth concerning the actual ancestors was to exert itself. The personification of history, which was the original purpose of genealogy, is still its greatest fascination, all the more so now that it is (or should be) dealing in scientifically proven facts. Tracing the history of one family is an admirable way of learning history. The reflection of wars and great national events on a set of individual families can sometimes tell one much more than the wide-ranging generalizations of a theorizing politico-economic historian; similarly how much deeper an understanding of social history can be derived by reading the plain facts about families without having them interpreted and analysed by a sociologist, incapable of thinking in anything but twentieth-century terms.

The twisting of facts to achieve a more pleasing result in a pedigree is as old as genealogy itself and still, regrettably, not unknown today. The biblical genealogies came to be dominated by the idea of purity of descent, illustrating the continuity of the race in exile. The first records in Greece were genealogical by nature, but open to abuse and of little historical value. Before the Roman Empire collapsed, the falsifying of patrician pedigrees back to Aeneas was a noted feature of that civilization. Busts of bogus ancestors would be placed in the shrines rather in the way that latter-day parvenus purchased their family portraits in antique shops.

The growth of genealogy took place as nations established themselves with modes of government and legal systems. Royal genealogies, as set out in the chronicle books, were obviously of the utmost importance in deciding the succession of kings and princes. The desire to assert the privileges of an aristocracy by birth was a powerful factor in Roman and Greek times (even in the days of the Republic) and in the development of genealogy throughout modern history. Inheritance is the heart of the hereditary principle and to settle disputes as to the inheritance of property, particularly real estate, genealogy came into its own.

The sixteenth century saw the start of collections of genealogies in manuscript and printed volumes; and the scholarship of the antiquaries of the seventeenth century uncovered material of immense value to the genealogist and demographer. Dugdale's prototype *County History of Warwickshire* and the work of the versatile Gregory King, the father of population studies, are outstanding examples of this period. Dugdale was also the first to produce, in his *Baronage*, a decent collection of the pedigrees of titled families. The eighteenth-century aristocratic view of genealogy is best summed up by Lord Chesterfield, commissioning, in a sarcastic gesture, portraits of Adam and Eve de Stanhope; and it was not until the nineteenth century that the pride of *Peerages* grew to such remarkable proportions. The 1700s had seen the appearance of *Collins's Peerage*, a largely legendary work which was corrected quite reasonably by Sir Egerton Brydges in its fifth edition (1778), apart from the insertion of his own forged ancestry. This is a characteristic syndrome of genealogists who, though reliable on other people's pedigrees, often get so hooked up on their own family trees that they alter records to suit their delusions of grandeur.

The nineteenth century was the golden age of bad genealogy; a whole shoddy industry, propped up by the pretensions of the parvenus to social status, supplied bogus evidence of gentility. There was also the craving for medieval romanticism, and to satisfy the families (the customers) some lamentable exercises in 'Gothick phantasie' were perpetrated. Mythological twaddle was put into the beginning of the pedigrees, which would often begin with the dread phrase 'The origins of this ancient family are lost in the mists of antiquity . . .'; whereas it was often more likely – social mobility being one of the key factors in tracing a genealogy – that the origins were lost in the dust thrown up by their carriage wheels. Genealogy became almost irredeemably tainted with the stigma of snobbery.

The twentieth century has been the age of the genealogy of the common man. Everyone has ancestors, and to a genealogist the fourteen generations behind Harold Wilson are of as much interest as those of the 14th Earl of Home. The Society of Genealogists was founded in 1911 to promote interest among amateur family historians; in 1968 the first professional body (the Association of Genealogists and Record Agents) was formed to establish codes of practice.

In 1974 the Federation of Family History Societies was founded, with the aims of co-ordinating and assisting the work of individuals as more and more people became involved in the search for their roots. Today the FFHS numbers nearly 200 member societies throughout the world.

Another burgeoning area in modern genealogy is the use of the personal computer to store, organize and present data and to communicate with other searchers, via the Internet. One aspect of this development is the publishing of personal family trees on the Internet. There is an ever-growing selection of software on the market which enables family information to be stored in an organized way and presented as 'pedigree charts', either horizontal in the American fashion or in the British 'drop-line' style. Care has to be taken to select a package which suits your own needs and hardware and which will be flexible enough to allow you to do some of the organizing.

Moreover, an increasing number of primary sources, such as census returns, are being transferred to CD-ROM, which greatly facilitates research. The Church of Jesus Christ of Latter-Day Saints has led the field in this respect and the collection of databases known as Family Search, which is available at the Family Records Centre and some family history centres (usually in Latter-Day Saints churches), includes computerized indexes to the International Genealogical Index, the collection of genealogies submitted to the LDS Church, and the catalogue to the vast Family History Library at Salt Lake City. However, the days when we can 'look it all up on the computer', or indeed 'download it all', are still a long way off.

GENEALOGY AND GENETICS

From the earliest times heredity was regarded as the most important factor in deciding a child's future. The reason for this was the observation that children often resemble their parents, and that brothers and sisters often resemble each other. This is particularly obvious in the case of identical twins, who are not only identical with respect to heredity, but also very similar indeed in their respective personalities and talents. Thus the study of heredity is closely linked with that of family history. Knowledge of genetics is growing constantly, and for a good up-to-date overview of the subject we recommend Steve Jones's books *The Language of Genes* (1993) and *In the Blood* (1996).

This way of looking at the origins of personality was supported by the fact that certain types of ability run in families. One has only to think of the Bach, Russell or Cecil families or the descendants of Josiah Wedgwood and Charles Darwin. But it is not at all clear why family resemblances should be interpreted in terms of heredity rather than environment. It is, indeed, possible that the outstanding qualities of the Bachs, Darwins, Cecils and Russells may have been transmitted through the exceptionally favourable environment the parents provided for their children and grandchildren. Conversely, the fate of children with feeble-minded parents may just as easily be explained in terms of unfavourable environment. It is clearly impossible to argue from the resemblance of children to their parents to the importance of either heredity or environment, simply because both these hypothetical causes would work in the same direction.

Studies of inheritance have revealed a phenomenon known as 'regression to the mean'. The children of exceptionally tall parents will be tall, but not quite so tall as their parents. The same applies to children with very short parents who will tend to be somewhat taller than their parents, though still below average height. This phenomenon is quite universal and has been found to obtain, not only in relation to physical characteristics, but mental ones as well, and intelligence, in particular, has been studied exhaustively in this respect. The children of very bright and very dull parents respectively regress to the mean. This regression also obtains in the field of personality, so that the children of exceptionally unstable or of extroverted parents will be more stable and more introverted than their parents.

The truth is that genetic factors may produce dissimilarities just as readily as similarities. Each time a man and a woman beget a

13

child, their genes are mingled in such a way as to produce a new and different combination which ensures that each individual is completely different from any other. Only identical twins have identical heredity. Brothers and sisters may be, and usually are, like each other, and may resemble their parents in some respects, but we can all point to people who are very unlike their parents and siblings. This is what would be predicted from our knowledge of the segregation of genes, and it is this dissimilarity that probably forms the strongest reason for asserting the importance of genetic factors. On the environmental hypothesis, brothers and sisters should be much more like each other than they usually are, especially if they have all enjoyed the same kind of home environment and upbringing. Environmental factors alone would not account for the very great dissimilarities often found between siblings who have been brought up together. Thus heredity produces both similarities as well as dissimilarities, and it is important to remember this when looking back on one's own family history.

It has often been asked how familial data can be used to substantiate the claim that heredity plays an important part in causing individual differences in intelligence. A knowledge of the degree of consanguinity between different types of kin makes it possible to deduce the precise amount of similarity that ought to be observable between them with respect to intelligence. Thus the highest degree of relationship should be found for identical twins; that between fathers or mothers on the one hand, and sons or daughters on the other, should be about half that seen for identical twins. The relationship between uncles and nephews, aunts and nieces should be smaller again, and so on. If genetic factors alone were the ones that were active, the degree of similarity should coincide with the degree of relationship. When this is done, observation comes close to theory, indicating that the effect of environment is not very strong. After all, the different members of a family enjoy broadly the same environment, yet the dissimilarities in IQ between them increase significantly the lower the degree of consanguinity.

Similar studies have been carried out with personality, in which identical and fraternal twins have been studied, and the outcome has usually been much the same. On the whole, genetic factors exert a powerful influence on the different aspects of personality and usually exceed that of environment, although the precise values depend upon the particular personality traits examined. The most convincing evidence for strong genetic determination is found in people's tendency to be sociable, impulsive and generally extrovert, as opposed to the contrary traits. Almost equally good evidence is available for emotional instability as opposed to sang-froid.

Another way of studying heredity and environment is by looking at the characters of adopted children. Those adopted in the first few months of life owe their biological inheritance to their true parents, but their environment is provided exclusively by their adoptive parents. The question arises whether they resemble their true parents more than their adoptive ones. The answer is simple. Adopted children are more like their true parents in intelligence and do not resemble their adoptive parents to any notable extent. This often leads to adoptive parents being disappointed, for they hope that by providing a good environment, they will be able to bring up their adopted children to the level of their own. Of course, they may be lucky, and find they have adopted a genius, but the bright child may be held back if the adoptive parents are dull or intellectually much inferior.

The inheritance of intelligence can be studied in the offspring of inbred families. Some genes are dominant, others recessive. Intelligence, being obviously useful, is likely to show dominance in its mode of inheritance. If any kind of inbreeding takes place, the children of such marriages will show an increase of dominant characteristics, some of which may be desirable while others are undesirable.

An equally important consideration relates to the question of assortative mating. In other words, birds of a feather tend to flock together: intelligent men tend to marry intelligent women. This powerfully increases the heritability of this particular characteristic. However, no such assortative mating can be demonstrated in the field of personality. Extroverts do not tend to marry extroverts more often than introverts; emotionally unstable people do not tend to choose neurotic partners more often than stable ones.

Given all these facts, genealogical investigations of single families, while having little or no scientific importance as such, can be all the more fascinating for the investigator who tries to discern in the pattern of family history the differing threads of heredity and environment. In individual cases these can never be conclusively demonstrated to be responsible for a particular characteristic, but we can reasonably argue from what is known about genetics to the individual case, and arrive at some plausible hypothesis about what, in our own make-up, we owe to our ancestors through the agency of genetics, and what through the agency of environment.

HANDWRITING

More often than not the only 'artefacts' a person leaves for posterity which have emanated from him personally and are in essence uniquely 'of him' are his handwritten records. Handwriting is a record of the individual expression of his personality, and can be studied in detail if it appears in diaries and letters, and any changes over the years can be observed. A handwriting consultant with good historical background and knowledge, who understands the milieu and the copy-books of the time, can build up a picture of someone who died hundreds of years ago. For example, the disturbed writing of King James I and the writing of the ill-fated King Charles I of the United Kingdom bring their personalities to life in relation to the way they affected the course of history.

The study of human personality from handwriting is called graphology. An interest in the connection between handwriting and personality recurs throughout history. Aristotle and the Roman historian Suetonius Tranquillus are quoted as having shown interest in the subject, the latter in *The Lives of the Caesars*. John Keats said in a letter, 'I am convinced more and more day by day that fine writing is next to fine doing, the top thing in the world.' Disraeli, Goethe, Robert Browning and Baudelaire all flirted with the subject, which was intermittently a fashionable intellectual pursuit in Europe at the time.

Handwriting fashions change like those of costume and architecture. They are shaped by the social climate and changes in taste reflecting the spirit of the times and also by the technology of the day and materials available. When paper was scarce and expensive it was cheaper to write with a stick in damp clay; when feathers were made into pens and the art of turning skins into vellum was discovered the style changed again. The ball-point pen has similarly changed modern writing radically. The thick, rounded letter-forms of the Carolingian hand which developed in France in the early Middle Ages changed imperceptibly into a more angular Gothic style at about the same time that round arches gave way to pointed ones in ecclesiastical and military architecture. Gothic, in turn, gave way during the Renaissance to a more flowing and graceful style influenced, no doubt, by the severe simplicity of the classical architectural forms which inspired the new movement. It is perhaps not insignificant that the Germans had a preference for the disciplined, iron-hard Gothic script right up to the time of Hitler.

In England a number of different 'hands' emerged around the middle of the sixteenth century. There was a native plain hand for correspondence, secretary hand and italic script for formal documents such as wills and parish registers, and court hand for legal documents, especially those written in Latin.

With the invention of the steel nib at the end of the seventeenth century, commerce and the law adopted copper-plate script which endured to the end of the nineteenth century and beyond. The early twentieth century saw the introduction of school copy-books written in a flowing, connected style with a rightward-moving slant and tall uppers with a confident look about them. This style admirably reflected the optimistic materialism, integrity and dedication of the great Empire-builders. Following the catastrophe of the First World War there was another significant change in writing style with the emergence of 'print script', an upright, disconnected and rounded style which did not lend itself to cursive elegance. Its introduction into the class-room was to herald the arrival of our uncertain modern age and of the utilitarian ball-point pen.

Today people write smaller than they did a century ago. Personalities tend to be smaller because they tend to specialize. In fashion both men and women favour jeans, and captions on films are often written without capital letters. Victorian corsets have been consigned to the flames along with bras, and handwriting, like architecture has lost its beauty in the cult of punk, lack of delight and overwhelming cynicism.

In the West we write from left to right, so in the field of handwriting the future, where we are going to, is on the right, the past, where we have come from, on the left. Lack of discipline and a sense of purpose for the future is reflected in a notable increase in 'left' tendencies, an increase in left-handedness and backward (or leftward) sloping writing. People are more concerned with the past and what has gone before; this is epitomized by the great popularity of historical spectaculars and what has loosely been called the nostalgia business. If we think of paternalism as being associated with the right (not necessarily in the political sense, of course), then maternalism can be associated with the left. It is significant, therefore, that we live in the age of the first British woman Prime Minister and of women's lib.

It can be seen that in families where correspondence and diaries have been kept, graphological examination of these documents can shed considerable light upon the characters of the people who wrote them.

Here is an example. Several dozen samples of writing covering five generations of a family were subjected to minute examination, in particular that of George, and his wife, Jane, and their son Simon. Simon was born when his two grandfathers were very old men, and he died before most of his grandchildren were born. Nevertheless it was possible to trace through these five generations certain characteristics. In the case of George, it was not possible to examine any examples of handwriting dating from the period before he met Jane, so any assessments had to be based on what survived from his maturity, and chiefly from the period 1873–82. Each sample differed in style, but one was of particular interest, for George apologizes to his wife 'for the manner in which this letter is written'. It is the only one written naturally. The writing reveals a personality who had a mental picture of himself built up in youth, from which he never deviated. George saw himself as strong, reliable and friendly, and believed himself possessed of great charm. He wished to present this image to the world, and believed that others must see him in this light. His writing showed that he was a man driven by his desire for stature and professional prestige. In private he had to be the focus of attention and admiration. He was an incurable optimist, but beneath this façade his self-confidence fluctuated alarmingly. He possessed drive and ambition, but lacked a goal and purpose in life. He was clear-minded and objective, passionate, greedy and sometimes deceitful. The constant effort of playing a part tended to make him muddle-headed and compromised his judgement.

None of this was apparent from the content of the surviving documents themselves. Jane's writing, on the other hand, showed that as she matured she acquired an ease of manner and regularity of behaviour which she lacked in youth. Considerably more documents in her handwriting survive, and considerably more was known about her personality from these. Nevertheless, her handwriting suggested that she became dominated by a material and physical possessiveness, amounting in later years to an emotional sickness. This was something which the contents of her letters did not reveal, although the handwriting most certainly did. Comparing the handwriting of George and Jane, one finds some interesting similarities, which suggests that in many respects they were birds of a feather. In their personal standards, interests and depth of feeling, the evidence of their writing suggests that they were compatible. Both appear calculating and money-minded, but in their respective attitudes to personal distance the seeds of friction can be detected.

Their son Simon was a man of exceptional ability, both artistic and practical. He was an inventor and the founder of a successful business. In extreme youth (and letters from his fifth year to his death have survived as well as a mass of notebooks of a technical nature) Simon's writing is remarkable for the drive and vision it reveals. Research into the childhood environment of famous and successful men has shown that one parent frequently possesses a taste for research, experimentation or adventure, and a need for physical or intellectual activity. It has also shown that a possessive and ambitious mother can channel her thwarted wishes into ambition for her son. An unresolved Oedipus complex can, therefore, be the source of energy whereby the son tries to make the mother happy, feeling it to be his mission to succeed where the father has failed.

19

George had been a photographer, and his father before him a musician. He had absolutely no business sense, and had eventually gone bankrupt. The grandfather, however, had been a man of European stature, though likewise lacking in business acumen. In Simon's childhood writing an unconscious pull towards his mother is very apparent; so is his strong desire to excel. From a very early age he possessed a great capacity for thinking big and long-term planning. The writing suggests an exceptional ability for getting things done and seeing them through to their conclusion. He appears exceptionally thorough, and had a tendency throughout his life to make doubly sure, and to return constantly to correct what he had previously written.

Simon was a man prepared to observe the conventions of his age, where other men of equally great originality might disregard conventionalities. He was less original as a thinker, though better able to see the potential in other people's ideas and to exploit them with great imagination. This element of conventionality is one which permeates his writing throughout his life, suggesting a wish to proceed by orthodox routes rather than to strike out into fields beyond his own sphere. The writing reveals some strange alternations in his character. On the one hand there is aggression, and on the other humanitarianism, a hard streak balanced by something almost amounting to gullibility, but resulting in an impressionable, easily accessible personality.

About 1884, at the age of twenty, certain changes in his writing began to appear, indicating a versatility of the mind within a set framework. Later these variations increase, reflecting, by 1890, a nervous stress and strain. The most striking feature is the appearance of a halo-like loop above the letter 'k'. This detached movement is a characteristic of the writing of his son Bernard and daughter Sarah, and can even be detected in an embryonic form in his own childhood writing as early as 1872, when he was eight. This and other unconscious features detected in Simon's writing and that of his children, can be clearly observed in the writing of his father and grandfather, suggesting that the origin of certain character attributes can be traced genetically from particular sources by a study of handwriting.

Many early records up to about the mid-eighteenth century are in Latin; and even English documents can be difficult to read because of abbreviations, flourishes and scripts; the main varieties are medieval court hand, secretary hand (sixteenth century onwards) and the italic hand (late seventeenth century onwards). Many county record offices and other organizations provide classes in palaeography (reading and transcribing old documents such as deeds and wills), and there are several books giving guidance, for example: Eileen Gooder, *Latin for Local History* (1978), L. C. Hector, *The Handwriting of English Documents* (1979), C. T. Martin, *The Record Interpreter* (1982). A good Latin dictionary is helpful, but more relevant is R. E. Latham, *Revised Medieval Latin Word-List* (1965).

2

SURNAMES: THEIR ORIGIN AND MEANING

◆

Ever since antiquity, one of the chief requirements of society has been the ability to distinguish individuals by their own name. Originally people had only one name, but as society became more complex, this name became peculiar to the person concerned. At the dawn of Roman history, individuals were given one name only, but with the development of Roman society, a system was perfected to distinguish individuals from each other which resulted in their having up to four names. The first of these was the *praenomen*, followed by the *nomen*, then by the *cognomen* and frequently by an *agnomen*. The *praenomen* was a personal name chosen from a fairly limited number, possibly not more than thirty, and was often repeated within the same family. Typical examples are Caius, Publius, Marcus, Lucius, etc.

The *nomen* indicated the clan or *gens*, and was carried by every male and female member of the same *gens*, even by adopted children and by freed men and foreigners who had become Roman citizens as a result of service to a particular *gens*. The *nomen* is the most important part of a Roman individual's name. It links him directly with his clan, and also to both his ancestors and descendants. It is the symbol of the unity and continuity of the clan. For example, the full name of the Roman Emperor Claudius – Claudius Nero Drusus Germanicus – tells us a good deal about his ancestry.

The *cognomen* or surname indicates divisions of the clan into various families, and in general originated from a physical or moral attribute. The *agnomen* was added to indicate a particular situation, quality or relationship of a person who had been adopted.

Roman society, therefore, perfected rules for the distribution and succession of names comparable to our present system, and which were not found anywhere else amongst the peoples of antiquity.

The Greeks, in contrast to the Romans, tended to give people somewhat fantastic names, or names which had an idealistic ring to them. Many Greek names end in -cles (glory or fame) e.g. Pericles (very glorious); Sophocles (famous for wisdom); Callicles (famous for beauty). Other names began with Cle- such as Cleophanes (radiant with glory). Many Greek names incorporate the word 'aristos' (the best) e.g. Aristophanes (radiant with the best, or emanating goodness).

Whereas these names tend to be poetic, noble, fantastic or idealistic, the Romans in rugged contrast favoured much more prosaic names derived from mundane sources; for example Agricola (farmer); Cicero (a man who grows peas – maybe a peanut farmer!); Porcius (pig breeder); Rufus (red); Longus (tall); Crassus (fat); Balbus (stammerer); Claudius (lame); Plautus (flat-footed); Calcus (blind); Scaurius (club-footed); the list is endless and almost as if culled from the orthopaedic unit of a hospital. The ultimate in prosaic names must surely be those derived from numbers, such as Secundus (second); Tertius (third); Quartus (fourth); Quintus (fifth); Sextus (sixth) and so on. These names even became diversified into Quintilianus, Sextius, Octavianus and so on. It is almost as if fathers could not be troubled to find names for their offspring, so just called them two, three, five or whatever.

An element present in Greek names, but only in a minor way, reflects religion and an awareness of God. In the countries of the Middle East, and especially amongst Arabs and Jews, names referring in some way to God are extremely common. Many Jewish names incorporate the syllable Ja, Jo or Je, short for Jehovah or Jahwe, and begin or end with El, both of which mean God. For example Joshua (whose help is God); Jokanaan (John) (whom God has given); Jehosaphat (to whom God has done justice); Obadaiah (in Arabic Abdullah – God's Knight); Elimelech (to whom God is King); Eliezer (to whom God is help); Nathaniel (God-given); and Joel (a double reference to God, i.e. God is Jehovah). Even abbreviated names such as Nathan, which is short either for Nathaniel or Jonathan, contain this God element.

Ancient Teutonic names likewise reflect the characteristics of that warlike race. A strong preoccupation with heroes, war and fighting distinguish the Germans of antiquity. War and a thirst for adventure according to Tacitus (far from silent as his name implies), were what the Germans were best known for, and the 'Furor Teutonicus' is reflected in their names. The words for weapon, war, struggle and victory are at the root of most ancient Teutonic names. *Hild, gund, had, bad* and *wig* are ancient Teutonic words for struggle, battle and war, which have disappeared from the German language as it is spoken today, but which entered Britain with the Angles and Saxons, and which survive today, as for example in Wyman from Wigmund, and Hathaway from Hadawig.

Germans, more than other European peoples, have tended to keep their ancient names. Names such as Otto, Hermann, Heinrich, Adelbert, Dietrich and Bernhardt are all of Teutonic origin. These names spread outwards from Germany and by the time of the Crusades they were found belonging to Frenchmen, Italians and Normans. For example Godfrey (Gottfried) de Bouillon, Robert of Normandy, Raymond of Toulouse, Boemund of Taranto. In 991, many of the French bishops who gathered at the Synod of Reims had German names; e.g. Adalbert of Laon, Godermann of Amiens, Odo of Senlis, Ratbod of Noyon and several others.

After the fall of Rome, it was not until the eleventh century that it was again felt necessary to distinguish individuals by more than one name or to distinguish every clan or stock by a surname. The *cognomen* or family surname which has now been incorporated legally into society originated towards the end of the tenth century. It is true, however, that a few great families were distinguished by surnames as early as the ninth century, but only a very few documents have come down to us from this remote period to show which names were used as surnames transmitted from father to son and which were used as second names or nicknames.

The essential characteristic of a surname is its continuous transmission from father to son indicating the stock from which a family descends. In Italy, the Venetians were the first to use surnames. A document dated 982 signed by Baduarius Bragadino, Vitalis Greco, Johannes Bembo, Dominicus Maurocene and Dominicus Contareno among others, is the earliest surviving example.

There must be tens of thousands of differently spelt British surnames, but their modern form is comparatively recent, often preserving a phonetic spelling found two or three hundred years ago in some parish register or manorial roll. Some British surnames sound very foreign; indeed a great many are of German, French, Scandinavian and Jewish origin. But the name Pharaoh, for example, has nothing to do with Egypt but is a reconstructed spelling of Faro, originally Farrer, found also as Farrey, Farrah (made famous by the manufacturers of Harrogate toffee) and Farrow. The Sussex name of Van Ness has as little to do with Holland as its variant Venis has to do with Venice. Both are variants of a French place name Venoix in Normandy, where one of William the Conqueror's knights held land before the Conquest. Other variants of this name appear as Veness and Venus – nothing to do with the erotic activity of one of its bearers.

People nowadays are very particular about the correct spelling of their surnames, but a fixed spelling has generally only been adopted since Victorian times, and one cannot therefore assume that a distinctive spelling found in the past and continued to the present indicates continuity of line. The whims of scribes and the dictates of fashion had more influence on the spelling adopted from time to time than any other factor, particularly as most people were illiterate and signed with a mark.

We are fortunate in the English-speaking countries that the custom – though not the law – has long been that the children of a marriage assume the father's surname. Certainly in England this has been the case since medieval times, but in Wales there was a system of patronymics until recent centuries by which there was one name for each generation, linked to the previous one by the appellation 'son of'. The Scottish and the Irish clan/sept systems have resulted in the suppression of Celtic surnames, the acquisition or imposition of substitutes, and the limitation to a clan name.

Thus a surname, better than any pedigree, can take one back in the male line over twenty generations or more and then back again, more indefinitely, as a byname or forename, perhaps, to a person of Saxon or Norman or even Danish origin.

Surnames became fixed and hereditary over a long period and were in common use from about the beginning of the sixteenth century. No laws were made on the subject (and there are still none) and there was no conscious decision in any one generation to adopt a surname and make it hereditary; it was all very much a matter of convenience, both personal and administrative. Before this time, as again is the custom now, 'Christian'-names sufficed for daily use.

Surnames may be divided into five main groups:

1. Surnames of relationship, that is to say deriving from the father's name (patronymic) or mother's name (matronymic) – Johnson, Alisson.
2. Surnames deriving from offices, titles, professions or trades – Judge, Lord, Parson, Tailor.
3. Surnames deriving from places or country of origin, from feudal fiefs and from topographical features – London, French, Ecclestone, Hill.
4. Surnames deriving from plants, fruits, flowers and animals – Quince, Bull, Tree. This is a particularly popular category among Italians, where an eccentric king of Naples once decided to award his courtiers titles of nobility, all of which were connected with vegetables, hence: Duca della Verdura (Duke of Greens), and Conte Carotti (Count Carrots).
5. Surnames deriving from nicknames – Cruickshanks, Goosey, Sharp, Wise. A sub-division of this category contains what may be termed phrase names, such as Purefoy – pure faith; Godsave or Godsalve. Such nicknames have the crudest of origins. There is the famous story told by John Aubrey in his *Brief Lives* of the courtier

who, on making a profound obeisance before Queen Elizabeth I, had the misfortune to break wind. He was so overcome with embarrassment that he went into voluntary exile for many years. On his return home it happened that the Queen met him on one of her Progresses. With a tact not perhaps as great as that of her latter-day namesake Elizabeth II, the Queen said 'Sir, we greet you. We have forgot the fart.' It was no doubt an ancestor who committed the same faux pas at the French Court, who earned for Marshal Pétain the name of Roland Le Péteur.

In the nineteenth century the fashion for multiple surnames began to appear. One of the earliest examples is Ashley-Cooper, dating from the late seventeenth century, but with the union of aristocratic or politically influential houses, the habit increased. When John Churchill, Duke of Marlborough, died without a male heir, his daughter combined her surname with her husband's to produce Spencer-Churchill. They were followed by the Cavendish-Bentincks, Montagu-Douglas-Scotts, Twistleton-Wykeham-Fiennes, Ernle-Erle-Drax and even Cave-Brown-Cave. Generally speaking this custom grew out of the wish to perpetuate the name of a family which would otherwise have died out for want of male heirs. In earlier times the surname was given as a first name, so that one can find in the sixteenth or seventeenth century such names as Bassing-bourne Gawdy, Moundeford Kirby, Seckford Gosnold, where the given name is usually that of the mother's family or more rarely the surname of a godparent from whom it was hoped the child would receive a substantial legacy. Nowadays the tendency is to drop one of the two surnames, as for example, the family of Lord Brabourne, the late Earl Mountbatten's son-in-law, who now call themselves Knatchbull, whereas they were formerly Knatchbull-Hugessen.

Some surnames that have disappeared in this country are still alive and well and flourishing in America and Australasia, while others have assumed different forms in those countries, particularly the United States, for a variety of reasons. Taken down by 'foreign' clerks, uttered by descendants unfamiliar with the place from which they originally hailed, if a locative name, they became distorted in the process and then formalized in this condition when spellings became fixed during the last century. Conversely, in many cases foreign names have accidentally or purposely become disguised as English names, so that now they cannot be told apart, with sometimes traditions or legends accruing to support their supposed origin, so that we are back again to the parallel of the modern Englishman who accepts unchecked family stories as to the origin of his own name and family. However, in general, the surnames of modern America reflect ethnic origins and though the United States and Canada are chiefly English-speaking, the names of their inhabitants reflect the polyglot nature of Europe.

3

WHERE TO BEGIN: FAMILY SOURCES AND TRADITIONS

The first rule for the family historian is this: always work from the known to the unknown. This is the principle adopted by all police forces the world over, because it is the one which produces results which stand up to the most critical examination in courts of law. This may, perhaps, seem a somewhat stark approach to family history, but if you wish to create a pedigree that truly records your ancestry and which is worth handing down to posterity, then it is essential.

Probably most of us have family legends of lost fortunes and vast acres that should by right belong to us. Many have been told of an ancestress who was 'taken advantage of' by the Duke of Blankshire, or that we really belong to the landed gentry, or have blue blood in our veins. Grandmother, for example, may be convinced that her husband, long since dead, was a descendant of, shall we say, the Percys. On investigation, however, it may turn out that he was only the son of a man who lived in Alnwick. It is indeed possible that the descent is genuine; on the other hand everything could be thoroughly above board and the only connection may turn out to be that of employer and employee.

A very large number of Americans are convinced that their ancestors came over the Channel with William the Conqueror, and over the Atlantic in the *Mayflower*. This is fascinating romantic stuff, but the genuine family historian should be seeking fact not fiction. Since a surprising number of people can genuinely trace their ancestry to King Edward III, the legend may not be so fanciful after all, but the point is it must be proved. Many traditions become exaggerated or diluted to become 'more acceptable', particularly the latter, for our Victorian ancestors were adept at locking skeletons in cupboards and sweeping dirt under carpets. It is therefore not advisable to accept everything at face value, yet traditions nevertheless carry a grain of truth, and should be borne in mind as they may help to point out a line of research which otherwise would be overlooked.

It is not always possible to establish a connection with a distinguished family of the same surname. This is a trap into which the descendants of many emigrants tend to fall. Howard, for example, is an extremely common surname, sometimes deriving from Hayward – an official found on every manor in the land – and sometimes from the old German for high or chief warden, and occasionally from the old French Huard which in turn derives from the old German, literally translated as brave heart. But because the premier English peer, the Duke of Norfolk, happens to have the surname Howard, people tend to jump to the conclusion that they are his kin. The chances of being related to such families is remote indeed. For names like Churchill, Townsend, Russell or Spencer derived in the first two instances from place names, Russell comes from red or 'russet', and Spencer from dispenser (of provisions), i.e. Steward or Butler. Indeed, what about Stuart and Boteler? If you are related to one of the prominent families bearing these names, the fact will automatically emerge in the course of research, and will be all the more rewarding for being accurate and substantiated by archival evidence.

Fortunately it is unnecessary to start research from such abstract points, for by applying the principle of working from the known to the unknown, the search is taken backwards generation by generation to the most remote ancestor the records can reveal. Having decided which particular surname is to be researched, initial enquiries will be directed towards one particular family. However, if you are undecided which line you wish to trace, it will be necessary to obtain as much information as possible from all branches of your family group. In this way it is possible to chart your genetic descent from both parents, four grandparents, eight great-grandparents and sixteen great-great-grandparents – always supposing you have that many. It is one of the ironies of genealogy that those with the bluest blood have the fewest ancestors, for the tendency among the aristocratic and dynastic families for cousins to marry each other reduces at a stroke the number of grandparents from four to two.

Those who attempt to trace their genetic ancestry frequently encounter the problem of a Jones, Smith or Brown ancestor, which effectively can block their path. At this point it is as well to pass on to a less common family surname, and undertake detailed research into that line instead. In practice, however, most family historians tend to keep to one surname only.

The most valuable and rewarding information will come from your eldest relatives, and it is logical to start by consulting them. If your surname is comparatively uncommon, it is often worth writing to people of the same name whose addresses you can find in the telephone directories. Some of these may well turn out to be remote cousins and they may have oral or documentary evidence to help in the building of a pedigree. As for family traditions, oral evidence is not always completely accurate, so allowance must be made for incorrect names, dates and places, which may have to be amended later when reliable documentary evidence is found.

An interesting example of this kind of problem relates to the American family of Langhorne. Family tradition, handed down over several generations, suggested that the family originated in the Welsh village of Laugharne and from a family of that name which owned large estates in Pembrokeshire in the seventeenth century. It is easy to see how this mistaken tradition arose, if one is unaware of the fact that the Welsh name is pronounced monosyllabically 'Larne'. The American family pronounces its name 'Langen' and the confusion arose from the mis-transcription of several documents in the printed Calendars of State Papers where a Colonel Richard Laugharne sometimes appears as Colonel Richard Langhorne. Anyone can be forgiven for confusing the written letters 'u' and 'n', and 'a' and 'o'. These were in fact two quite distinct families and it was not very difficult to disentangle the confusion once it was realized how the initial mistake had arisen.

Family Bibles are a most valuable source of evidence, for the records of births, christenings, marriages and deaths were usually made at or near the time of the event, and are therefore usually reliable. It is important, however, to check when the Bible was printed, for it is by no means unknown for the original Bible to disintegrate with wear and to be replaced by a new one, and for the entries either to be incorrectly transcribed or even entered from memory.

Copies of birth, marriage and death certificates may be found among family documents. Associated with these certificates may be baptismal certificates, wedding invitations and memorial cards, and because these are printed close to the time of the event, they are usually accurate records. The same applies to Confirmation and First Communion certificates, Barmitzvah cards, marriage contracts and settlements, and divorce settlements.

Records of academic and professional attainments are useful sources of information, particularly service records such as discharge papers. School prizes and certificates, university degrees, sporting prizes and cups, certificates of ordination, club and association records, trade union cards, apprenticeship indentures, trade and guild records, freedoms of cities, testimonials, civic awards, medals and decorations – all these add flesh to the bare bones of a pedigree and give clues to age and hence date of birth. In addition to these basic facts, they indicate abilities, interests and achievements in a way no other sources do. They can also point to the direction from whence some of your own interests and characteristics derive.

Records relating to property are valuable for the light they throw on the movements of a family from one place to another. Maps, passports, identity cards, denizations, naturalizations and letters, both personal and official, provide much information about a family, for they record major events in the lives of the individuals and families concerned.

Another type of record relates to wealth and health. These include bank books, stocks and share certificates, annuity (tontine) certificates, medical certificates, driving and other licences.

Finally, there are personal documents and mementos which may include pedigrees or notes on aspects of the family's history, which if not authenticated by a body such as the College of Arms, will need checking for accuracy. In this category fall diaries, personal letters and scrapbooks which, if subjected to handwriting analysis (see Chapter 1) can add greatly to one's knowledge of the character of the writers. Birthday books and cards, account books, book plates, samplers, which frequently include the age of the person who worked them and where and when they were made, armorial silver, china and glass, mourning and signet rings, seals and fobs, and of course portraits and photographs of people and houses are all very valuable. As an example of the way in which a picture of a house can help, a Canadian had a picture of a Georgian house in Somerset in his family album. It was taken about one hundred years ago, and the caption underneath it included the name of the house and the words 'God Bless our Home'. There was no one in the family who knew why it was in the album, nor the name or the relationship of the person who put it there. A letter to the present owner elicited a number of interesting facts, including copies of the deeds from which it was possible to discover that the house had been let for twenty years between 1860 and 1880 to a family which, on investigation, proved to have been that of one of his great-grandparents, whose name he did not even know. From this it was ultimately possible to discover when this particular individual had been born, married and emigrated, and why.

Naturally, a number of these items could be in the possession of distant members of the family, possibly those who descend from female lines and whose surnames are different from your own. Care should be taken when approaching such people not to give the impression that as the family historian of your particular branch, you are the person to whom they should belong. Whenever possible, offer to have the material copied at your own expense, or make arrangements to photograph it yourself. Since much research of this kind must be carried on by correspondence, often with elderly people who may be easily bothered by receiving letters asking numerous questions, and who may not be in the habit themselves of writing long letters, the response may be negative. Wherever possible it is a good idea to seek a meeting, and to record your conversation on tape. An excellent example of this technique is to be found in Ronald Blythe's marvellous book on Suffolk village life *Akenfield*, which is almost entirely based on tape-recorded interviews. When approaching people for family information, it is advisable to take or send a separate pedigree of the family group, and ask for comments, corrections and additions where appropriate. Ask if there are any documents available for copying, and if your correspondent knows of any other members of the family who might have information to offer. Always enclose a stamped addressed envelope or two International Reply Coupons.

If you do not know of any direct contacts, but know the town or county from which your ancestor came, then an enquiry through the personal column in the appropriate local newspaper or county 'countryside' magazine could bring results. Head the advertisement with the surname you are researching in bold type. Most people stop to read anything about their own name, or one that is well known to them. Follow this with a brief explanation of the research project, asking anyone with information or similar interest to contact you at the address shown. If the surname is a common one locally, much of the information may be irrelevant, on the other hand it may put you in touch with distant kinsfolk who are unknown to members of your family.

Modern scholarly work on surname origins has done much to dispel some of the wilder etymological guesses of the early surname dictionaries, notably the work of the English Surnames Survey, edited by R. A. McKinley, formerly of the Department of Local History at the University of Leicester. The six published volumes cover the West Riding of Yorkshire, Norfolk and Suffolk, Oxfordshire, Lancashire, Sussex and Devon. This is certainly a field in which there is much more work to be done.

4

PRINTED SOURCES

After getting all the information you can from family sources, and before embarking on extensive research in manuscript archives, it is wise to find out whether any work has been done before on the families in which you are interested, or whether anyone else is currently engaged in research with whom you might exchange information.

Two useful books available at most principal libraries are G. W. Marshall's *The Genealogist's Guide*, and J. B. Whitmore's *A Genealogical Guide* which is a continuation of Marshall's work. These books form a valuable index to pedigrees of three generations in the male line that have appeared in print before 1953. T. R. Thomson's *A Catalogue of British Family Histories* and G. B. Barrow's *Genealogist's Guide* are more recent works containing additional information which complement Marshall and Whitmore. Margaret Stuart's *Scottish Family History*, Joan P. S. Ferguson's *Scottish Family Histories held in Scottish Libraries* and Edward MacLysaght's *Irish Families, Supplement to Irish Families* and *The Surnames of Ireland* are the appropriate works for those countries.

Many other important works containing biographical material can be found in local reference libraries, such as *The Victoria County History of England*; the *Dictionary of National Biography*, *Who Was Who*, *Debrett's Peerage*, *Burke's Peerage* and *Walford's County Families*. *Burke's Family Index* (1976) provides a useful index to the titled and landed families in the Burke's Peerage publications.

County record offices and local study centres also have collections of local family histories, which are almost invariably indexed. There is also a large collection of family histories and pedigrees at the Society of Genealogists in London, which houses the largest specialized library on the subject in Britain. Non-members can make searches in the society's library for a daily fee.

If you have found, or think it likely, that the family you are researching is among the minority which is documented in printed sources, it may be worth consulting the catalogue of the British Library or one of the other copyright libraries: The Bodleian, Oxford, the Cambridge University Library, the National Libraries of Wales and of Scotland, and Trinity College, Dublin. Under the Copyright Act, a copy of every book published in Great Britain since 1814 must be sent to each of these six repositories. It may be possible to order a copy of a printed book that interests you through the inter-library loan scheme at your local public library. The Manuscript Department British Library also houses many of the unpublished family papers, diaries, genealogies and the huge collection known as the Harleian Manuscripts which includes copies of many of the pedigrees taken at heraldic visitations, extended by subsequent historians.

Many pedigrees, not all of them armigerous, are registered at the College of Arms in London, or at the Lord Lyon Court in Edinburgh, the two official bodies with jurisdiction over the granting of arms in England and Scotland. The corresponding body in Ireland is the Office of the Chief Herald of Ireland at Dublin Castle. The College of Arms does not allow public access for research, but searches can be undertaken by officers of the college on the payment of a fee. In Edinburgh and Dublin the registers are open to the public.

Another printed source of a very different nature should also be mentioned: the *Genealogical Research Directory* (in book form or CD-ROM), which is published annually and available at most local reference libraries, provides an alphabetical index of research interests submitted by individuals or groups, the addresses of whom are supplied.

5

CIVIL REGISTRATION

No matter how much information has been obtained from family and printed sources, the exciting time will come when you have to embark on original research of your own. For the family historian the progression of research is in the main logical so long as the axiom of working from the known to the unknown is adhered to. Inevitably the first public records required to extend a family history are those of civil registration of births, marriages and deaths.

The starting date for civil registration was not uniform throughout the United Kingdom. In England and Wales it started on 1 July 1837, and the country was divided into Registration Districts under the control of a Superintendent Registrar whose records contain all the original certificates for the events that were registered within that district. At the end of each quarter – March, June, September and December – copies of all registered events are sent to the Registrar General at the Office for National Statistics (General Register Office, formerly at St Catherine's House, London). These are collated into master indexes for births, marriages and deaths for the respective quarters, but it must be emphasized that the entries in them relate to when the event was registered, and not to the date it actually took place. If therefore you are looking for an event that happened near the end of a quarter, it may not be registered until the beginning of the next one.

Anyone can examine the quarterly indexes of births, marriages and deaths at the Family Records Centre, 1 Myddelton Street, London EC1R 1UW.

The distinctive bindings of the indexes – red for births, green for marriages and black for deaths – make it easy to locate the section required. Within each volume, all entries are arranged in strict alphabetical order. Because surnames are liable to variant spellings, however, it is advisable to make a list of all these so that each can be checked if the entry required cannot be located where you expect to find it. For example, a family named Langman might be indexed under Longman. The name Kirby can be spelt more than thirty ways phonetically. Because the letter 'b' in seventeenth-century script can be mistaken for 's' and 's' can be mistaken for 'f' the name could appear (and, indeed, has) as Kersie and Kerfitt, for 'tt' can be mistaken for a final 'e'.

You should start by looking at the volume where you think you will find the entry of your known family member. When you have found the volume you require for the appropriate quarter and year, and the particular name of the person you are looking for, it will then be necessary to note the various references shown against that name. The full entry indicates the surname, forename(s), registration district and the volume and page number on which the actual entry is recorded. This information, together with the year and quarter, are required for completing the application form to obtain a copy of the full certificate. You will need the full certificate as the short one is of little value for genealogical purposes, since it omits details of parentage and gives the date and place of birth only.

There are certain 'peculiarities' for each main section of the indexes which are worth noting. The indexes from the September 1837 quarter to the December 1865 quarter are handwritten on vellum and are split into a number of alphabetical volumes (a note of caution: these can be very heavy to handle). The details given are as previously described. Unless there are more than three, each forename is written out in full. In the year 1866 the indexes are printed, and for this year only the second and any other forenames are only shown by initials. From 1867 to 1911 these indexes are printed with most of the forenames.

In 1911 we witness the beginning of typescript indexes with again only the first forename being shown. All these indexes are now also available on microfiche, and the fiches are available at many county record offices, as well as the Society of Genealogists. In 1991 the actual records were transferred to Southport, the indexes remaining in London.

BIRTH

While the registration of marriages and deaths could rarely be avoided, there was no penalty for non-registration of birth before 1875; thus births before this date, and sometimes after, were often not recorded centrally. From 1912 onwards, the surname of the mother is recorded in the birth indexes, immediately following the surname and forename(s) of the child. This can be a valuable check that the entry is the correct one, provided, of course, that the mother's surname is known. This is also helpful in compiling a family group from the index entries without the expense of obtaining certificates for all the children born to a particular family. Some mothers' surnames are the same as the surname of the child. Although this can be a case of marriage between cousins, it quite frequently signifies a birth out of wedlock.

The information shown in each full birth certificate is as follows:

1. When and where born;
2. Name, if any;
3. Sex;
4. Name and surname of father;
5. Name, surname and maiden surname of mother;
6. Occupation of father;
7. Signature, description and residence of informant;

8. When registered;
9. Signature of registrar;
10. Name entered after registration.

If at the time of registration the forename(s) of the child have not been decided, the 'Name, if any' column will be left blank, and the entry in the index will show the surname, followed by either 'male' or 'female'. However, if the forename(s) were ultimately notified to the registrar, then they would be recorded in the last column, headed 'Name entered after registration'.

If the child was born out of wedlock, in most cases the name of the father is not shown, and the child is registered under the surname of the mother. However, since 1875 the father's name may be inserted, in which case the birth is registered under both surnames.

If the mother had previously been married, then the column 'Name, surname and maiden surname of mother' would show, for example, Jane Brown, late Smith, formerly Jones. But if the informant did not reveal this information, it will not be shown, and could therefore read Jane Brown, formerly Jones.

If you cannot find the entry of the person required in the main index, but other members of the family group are known, it is worth looking for one of these entries, and, if you find it, obtaining the certificate, as this will provide you with the information regarding the parents. This procedure is recommended because of the surname variants previously mentioned, which, apart from phonetic misinterpretation, can be caused by incorrect copying from the original registration.

MARRIAGES

Before 1912, the quarterly marriage indexes do not cross-reference brides and grooms, who are listed alphabetically under their respective surnames. The only information given in the indexes is the name of the bride or groom, the registration district and the reference number. To locate a particular marriage, therefore, the various entries for the two names have to be cross-checked until a matching pair is found. With marriages, both parties are indexed under their respective surnames; therefore it is always essential to check both the entries (assuming both surnames are known), in order to obtain the certificate, the district, volume and page number for both parties must be identical. Here sometimes one has to search a number of years if your particular ancestor was the youngest of a large family. Do not despair if you do not find a marriage quickly.

In the marriage indexes the surname of the other party is also shown after 1912. This again is a check that the entries are correct, if both surnames are already known.

Full marriage certificates contain the following information:

1. When married;
2. Name and surname of both parties;
3. Ages;
4. Condition (bachelor, spinster, widow, etc.);
5. Rank or profession;
6. The residence of both parties at the time of marriage;
7. Fathers' name and surname;
8. Occupation of fathers.

If the names of both parties are known, then it will be easier to locate the relevant index entry for the less common surname first, and then cross-check this with the other party's index entry for the matching references previously mentioned. If the bride is a widow her surname will be that of her late husband; but if a divorcee then it may be her previous married surname or her maiden name. Sometimes a woman has been living with her husband before the marriage, and may have changed her name to his by Deed Poll. Consequently she will be listed in the index under her changed, but lawful surname, and if declared at the time of registration, also under her original surname.

If the name of one or the other or both fathers is missing on the full certificate, this may be due to several reasons: the party was born out of wedlock, the father was deceased, or at the time of registration the information was not recorded. The last two instances are cases of negligence, but such cases are known to have happened. Some marriage certificates will show the name of the father together with the word 'deceased'. There is, therefore, no point in looking for his death registration after the day on which the marriage took place. On the other hand, the fact that 'deceased' is not recorded on the certificate is not proof that the father was in fact alive, as at the time of registration this particular question may not have been asked.

The ages shown on marriage certificates can be misleading. They may have been increased or decreased at the whim of the parties involved. Unfortunately, many are recorded as 'of full age', meaning that the people were twenty-one years old or upwards. Often '21 years' can indicate the same thing, merely that the person was of full age. 'Of full age' does not always mean that the person was twenty-one or over – it occasionally means the person was of the legal marriage age (until 1929, twelve for girls and fourteen for boys). The 'Residence at the time of marriage' may not always be the usual place of abode of the bride and bridegroom, but may be a temporary address of convenience. It is well worth noting the religion and occupation shown on marriage certificates, since these may be important clues to other records, and to the identification of people elsewhere.

DEATH

The death indexes show the age at death, after the forename(s) from 1866 to 1968. After 1969, the date of birth of the deceased is shown instead of the age at death, which may or may not be accurate.

Death certificates contain the following information:

1. When and where died;
2. Name and surname;
3. Sex;
4. Age;
5. Occupation;
6. Cause of death;
7. Signature, description, and residence of the informant;
8. When registered;
9. Signature of registrar.

It should be remembered that the place of death may not be the usual residence of the person who has died. In fact you may find that the deceased died many miles away from home. This can be helpful if he was visiting relations at the time, since it could guide you to an area from which the family originally migrated.

The age given can be incorrect and allowance must be made for this when calculating the probable year of birth. It is of course very helpful if the informant is a relative as the relationship may be stated which can confirm a tentative link in your research.

All certificates show places of residence, and if the events occurred near the date of a census, they offer a useful clue for searches in the returns immediately following or preceding them. Although the records of births, marriages and deaths registered in England and Wales since 1 July 1837 are the main class of records held by the Registrar General, there are others which are worth noting. Records of still-births registered in England and Wales since 1 July 1927 can be obtained only with the special permission of the Registrar General. Records of births and deaths at sea (known as the Marine Register Books) since 1 July 1837 relate to persons born on British ships whose parents were born in England and Wales. Records of births and deaths in aircraft began in 1949 (known as Air Register Books) and relate to these events occurring in any part of the world in any aircraft registered in Great Britain and Northern Ireland. Service records contain births, marriages and deaths among members of the armed forces and certain other persons, or occurring on board certain ships and aircraft. Royal Air Force Returns began in 1920. The registers of the Army are in two series. Firstly, there are the straightforward registers of Army records and chaplains' returns, and secondly there are the indexes of Regimental birth registers. Equally there are the equivalent registers of marriages and deaths which are not indexed but can be sought on personal application in the foreign department of the Office for National Statistics. There are also separate death registers of officers and men who died in the Boer War and Second World War for each of the services.

Entries of births, marriages and deaths for civilians which took place in foreign countries can be found in either the Consular

Records which are kept at the General Register Office or the Miscellaneous Records which are held at the Public Record Office. These comprise what is known as the Overseas Section which is probably the most apt term for describing a group of registers made up from various sources.

The Consular registers were started in 1849 by an Act of Parliament and continue until the present day. Miscellaneous registers are non-statutory ones which were sent into the Registrar General. They have now been sent to the Public Record Office and both the indexes and the registers can be seen at Kew unless they are less than thirty years old. The earliest of these are registers of births, marriages and deaths that took place at The Hague from 1627. There are also some eighteenth- and nineteenth-century records which begin before 1849. If you fail to trace your particular family in the Consular registers, then you should consult the Miscellaneous register.

Records for anyone born in one of the former or existing British Colonies are held by the Registrar General of that country except for those records held by the India Office at the British Library for British citizens born in India before 1947.

The last registers to be mentioned here are of British persons, civil or military, in the Ionian Islands from 1818–64 who were in either Cephallonia or Corfu.

Records of adoption consist of entries made in the Adopted Children Register, in accordance with the Adoption Acts, since 1 January 1927, and relate only to adoptions effected under these Acts.

In recent years the fee for full certificates has changed so frequently that it is advisable to ascertain the current charges from the Registrar General at the time of undertaking your research. Applications by post will be undertaken but the cost is currently more than double that of going to the General Register Office in person. Fees for searches are given in the free leaflet available from the Registrar General. The fee for each certificate obtained in person from the ONS in London is £6.50; postal applications at a higher fee (giving full references from the indexes) may be made to the ONS at Smedley Hydro, Birkdale, Southport PR8 2HH. If you cannot search the indexes yourself, you may also apply to Southport for a search.

Divorce records in England and Wales date back to 1852. However, it is necessary to know full particulars of names and the approximate dates of the Decrees Nisi and Absolute. Applications for the Decree Absolute should be made in person or by post to the Divorce Registry in London.

Apart from the obvious information obtainable from certificates, there are a few points worth noting which could also be of use. A note should be kept of all witnesses and informants that are shown on certificates as they could be relatives or provide links with other evidence for future research. It is possible that a few events were not registered, especially births, and the possibility is greater before 1875 because from that date the penalties for non-registration were increased. If, even after trying all possible surname variants, the search in the general indexes fails to produce results, then the period of search should be extended progressively either side of the expected date of the event. If the district where the event took place is known, it is advisable to try the district Superintendent Registrar's Office, in case of errors or omissions in the general indexes. Lastly, it may be that the event took place abroad, in which case either occupation or family connections may provide a clue for further research.

THE CHANNEL ISLANDS AND THE ISLE OF MAN

In the Channel Islands civil registration is divided between Jersey and Guernsey, each having their respective Registrars General. In Jersey, births, marriages and deaths have been recorded since August 1842, and information about them can be obtained from the Superintendent Registrar in St Helier, Jersey, but research enquiries should be addressed to the Société Jersiaise, St Helier.

The States of Guernsey has jurisdiction over the islands of Guernsey, Alderney, Brecqhou, Herm, Jethou and Sark. Registration of births and deaths is now governed by an Order-in-Council of March 1935 and registration of marriages by an Order-in-Council of May 1919. For the period before this, but after 1840, completed registers are held by the Registrar General in St Peter Port, Guernsey. It should be noted that some of the registers of Alderney were lost during the German occupation in 1940–45.

In the Isle of Man the statutory records of births and deaths relate to those registered since 1878 and marriages since 1884. In addition there is the Adopted Children Register which covers legal adoptions registered since 1928. Search fees are very reasonable and enquiries should be made to the Civil Registry, Douglas, Isle of Man.

6

CENSUS RETURNS

The census returns have been described by some researchers as the most helpful and revealing records that the family historian is likely to encounter. As early as 1750 it was proposed that regular censuses of the population should be held, but it was not until 1801 that they were introduced. Since that date they have been held every ten years with the exception of 1941. Unfortunately the returns up to and including 1831 are generally of little use from the family historian's point of view as the names of residents were not recorded. It is therefore those from 1841 onwards that are of interest. In England and Wales the census returns are not available for public inspection until they are over one hundred years old.

Census records of England, the Channel Islands and the Isle of Man may be consulted at the Family Records Centre, 1 Myddelton Street, London EC1 IUW, and also (usually) at the record office of the relevant county.

It is at this stage in your research that the addresses revealed by previous work can be of such value. The nearer the date on the records which reveal such addresses is to the date of each census, the greater the possibility that the person being sought will be found at that address when the census was taken.

The census of 7 June 1841 records the parish or township, and the name of the city, borough, town or village at the head of each enumeration sheet. The columns beneath show:

1. The name of the street, place or road and the name or number of the house;
2. The name and surname of each person in the house;
3. Age and sex;
4. Rank, profession or occupation;
5. Whether born in the same county;
6. Whether born in Scotland, Ireland or foreign parts.

The ages and persons under fifteen years are stated exactly, but those above fifteen years are rounded down five years, i.e. someone aged sixty-four appears as sixty, twenty-three as twenty, and so forth. Places of birth are indicated by 'Y' (Yes) or 'N' (No) and 'S' (Scotland), 'I' (Ireland), 'F' (Foreign parts) in the appropriate columns.

The returns of 1851, 1861, 1871, 1881 and 1891 are far more informative. They show the following additional information:

1. The schedule number;
2. Relationship to the head of the family;
3. Condition or matrimonial status;
4. The exact age of each person;
5. The exact parish and county of birth;
6. Whether deaf, dumb or blind.

In the 1871 census, provision was made to show if any person was an imbecile, idiot or lunatic. The dates on which the censuses were taken are important: 7 June 1841, 30 March 1851, 7 April 1861, 2 April 1871, 3 April 1881, 5 April 1891.

It must be noted that those listed in the census returns are every person living in the house on the day in question, together with those engaged at their labour during the night, and returning regularly next morning. No member of a household who normally slept away from the house was included, such as domestic staff, residents at an institution, and so on. Such persons would be recorded on the appropriate enumerator's return, at such places as hotels, lodging houses, hospitals, institutions, aboard ships, and even in tents. Visitors and servants are often listed in the household and their places of birth are worth noting as there may be some form of family connection in that area. Occupations are frequently abbreviated, e.g. Ag. Lab. for agricultural labourer; F.S. for female servant; Ind. for independent means; and so on.

The marks made by the enumerators after a list of names for a given address are to indicate, / the end of a household, and // the end of all households within the building. On some returns, particularly those for small villages, the name of the street or road is not shown, and the only identification given is that of the schedule number. To ascertain the likely location of the house or building concerned it will be necessary to check the 'description of enumeration district', which is to be found at the beginning of each such section of the census return. In any case, you can save many hours of searching by checking the description of each district first, to see if the street or road is listed as part of that particular enumeration. If it is not found, then each subsequent district should be checked until the place required is located. Roads of great length are invariably part of more than one district, in which case all districts may have to be checked before the required address is found. Sometimes an address cannot be found, owing to a change of house name or number, or even the name of the road itself, between the date on the source of information and the date of the census. In such cases, the record office should be consulted in order to find out whether a list of such changes exists for that particular locality. For large towns and cities, street indexes are available, and these are of considerable help in locating the section of the census return required to find a particular address.

It is also worth searching the area in the vicinity of the family residence. In the past, members of the same professions and family groups often lived near to each other, and the returns, by noting the trades or professions of those living in a locality, shed a great deal of light upon its social make-up. It must be stressed that the information recorded in the census returns is subject to varying degrees of error. False statements were made by those who had something to hide, or were just being awkward. Ages can be found to be only approximate; there is also the perpetual problem of surname variants due to spelling or phonetic misinterpretation.

Nicknames, stage names and noms-de-plume are sometimes found in census returns. In one case the individual's given name was Ernest but he was always known in the family as George because he liked this name better. Unless one has information of a private character it is usually impossible to identify such people with certainty, and much confusion is caused thereby. Bella for Isabella, Nelly for Helen and similar variants are very common and frequently found in returns.

Census returns are available for public inspection only if over one hundred years old, so the latest census available at present is that of 1898, and the 1901 census should be released in 2002. Nevertheless, it is possible to obtain from the ONS information on a named individual at a known address from the 1901 census, as long as you are next of kin or a direct descendant. An application form may be obtained from the Census Division at the Office for National Statistics, Segensworth Road, Titchfield PO15 5RR. You will have to provide the subject's full name, the address where he or she is thought to have been living, and your own relationship to the subject. The only information that will be released is the person's age and birthplace. The fee for this service is £40 including VAT at present.

The entire 1881 census of England, Wales and Scotland has been indexed by county on microfiche; these indexes show each individual, the age, birthplace, head of the household and full reference, which can then be followed up in the full return. There are also many indexes to other census years, usually on the basis of registration districts. For details consult Gibson and Hampson, *Marriage, Census and Other Indexes for Family Historians* (Federation of Family History Societies) which is regularly updated. The workings of the census are explained more fully in Higgs, *Making Sense of the Census* (PRO 1989).

7

PARISH,
NONCONFORMIST
AND ROMAN
CATHOLIC RECORDS

<><

At this stage of research, the accumulated evidence from certificates and census returns will provide the names of your ancestors and the approximate dates of events and places where they were living in the early nineteenth century or late eighteenth century. It is at this stage that the records of the parish and its administration will provide the main sources for these and earlier generations.

Of the many parish records available for research, undoubtedly the Parish Registers are the most important. The earliest registers in England and Wales began in 1538 when Thomas Cromwell, Vicar General to Henry VIII, issued an injunction that records of baptisms, marriages and burials should be kept by the clergy of the Church of England. These early registers are generally paper books, and few originals have survived. It is estimated that from more than 11,000 ancient parishes less than seven hundred have registers that go back to 1538. The remainder have registers that begin at various dates between then and 1597, and some even later than that. It was in 1597 that, for their safer keeping, parchment registers were ordered to be kept and that the earlier entries in the paper registers should be copied into them. Unfortunately the wording of the Act which referred to the copying of the earlier registers included the phrase 'but especially since the first year of Her Majesty's reign' (1558). This provided a loophole for the lazy who were looking for an excuse to limit copying to forty rather than sixty years. The Act also provided for transcripts to be made from the registers within a month after Easter for the previous year for submission to the bishop's registrar. These transcripts are generally known as Bishop's Transcripts and are usually deposited in the Diocesan Record Office. The original Parish Registers come in a great variety of shapes and sizes, but of more interest is the way in which they were written up. Most of the details of an event would be made in a notebook or on slips of paper by the incumbent or parish clerk and, according to the size of the parish, entered into the register later at various intervals, when they remembered. It does not, therefore, need much imagination to see that as a result of this custom, some events were either lost, written up from memory, or entered in the register out of chronological sequence. This, together with the fact that some registers were divided into three sections – baptisms, marriages, burials – others in chronological order with the events mixed according to the sequence in which they happened, and yet others used three separate registers, means that very thorough and careful checks must be made during research, unless the registers have been completely transcribed and indexed.

During the Commonwealth (1648–60) many clergymen were forced to leave their parishes, especially if they were Royalists. Some took their registers with them, some buried them for safety with the result that many were lost or irreparably damaged, and other registers were destroyed when Cromwellian soldiers plundered the churches. From September 1653 until the Restoration, Parish Registers (i.e. registrars) were appointed to record births, marriages and deaths with the Justice of the Peace to perform civil marriages. In some parishes the registers were well maintained, some to an even better standard than under the old system. In the majority of parishes, however, the standard deteriorated drastically and there are many instances where no records were kept at all during the whole period.

Due to the serious decline of the English wool trade, an Act was passed in 1678 that all the dead were to be buried in wool with a fine being imposed for non-compliance and an affidavit was made by a relative or associate of the deceased. Consequently 'Affid' or 'Affdt' can often be seen after a burial entry in the register. The Act was repealed in 1814, but had ceased to be enforced long before that date.

In 1694 'for carrying on the war against France' a duty was levied on a sliding scale for non-paupers of 2*s*. for a baptism or birth, 2*s*. 6*d*. for a marriage, and 4*s*. for a burial, rising to the considerable sum of £30 for the baptism of a duke's eldest son, and £50 for a duke's marriage or burial. The duty was abolished a few years later as it proved to be unenforceable.

During the eighteenth century both the Church and the State were concerned about the increasing laxity in performing marriages by clergymen who had been conducting ceremonies with scant regard to the status of both brides and grooms. This state of affairs was resolved in 1754 by Lord Hardwicke's Marriage Act which introduced separate marriage registers on printed forms which required the entries to be signed by the officiating minister, the bride and groom and two witnesses. The Act also reinforced the requirement that all marriages must be preceded by the calling of banns, for three successive weeks, unless a licence was granted, and marriages were only to be solemnized in a parish church.

The only exceptions to this rule were marriages of Quakers and Jews, since their records were considered satisfactory, and they were therefore allowed to continue conducting their own marriage ceremonies.

Hardwicke's Marriage Act did not eliminate clandestine marriages. Determined couples made for Gretna Green and other places across the Scottish border and for the Channel Islands, where the regulations were less stringent than in England.

Marriage licences and banns are a subject of importance. The great majority of British marriages were by banns (or 'proclamation'). The couple's intention to marry was announced on three Sundays in their parish churches – or between 1653 and 1660, it could be proclaimed in the nearest market-place on three market-days – to allow anyone knowing of any 'just impediment' to declare it.

Licences, however, were issued by the Church authorities, and these enabled people to marry immediately without banns. Apart from the obvious human need for a hasty marriage those who used them were the prosperous, who wanted to avoid publicity; soldiers and sailors who might be called away at short notice and had no home parish anyway where banns could be called; anyone whose freedom to marry needed to be clarified or (before about 1700) who wanted to marry at the religious seasons of prohibition (Lent, Advent, etc.).

The records (if they exist) of a marriage licence were the 'allegation', a declaration on oath by the bride and bridegroom of their freedom to marry; the 'bond', a record of security given by, usually, a close friend or relation of the truth of this; the 'licence', a document authorizing marriage, often at a stipulated church; finally there was often a register kept of the licences issued.

Licences were normally issued by bishops and archdeacons, or their officials, and the records are among the other archives of those dignitaries. However, where the parties to be married lived in different bishoprics, then strictly the licence should have been issued by the archbishop, although this rule was often broken.

The Stamp Act of 1783 imposed a duty of 3*d*. on all entries in Parish Registers, which was extended two years later to cover Nonconformists. As paupers were exempt, an increasing number of ordinary citizens declared themselves as such in order to avoid the duty. Once more, many poor people failed to have their children baptized. As before, this second attempt to raise revenues through the Parish Registers failed, and the Act was repealed in 1794.

The final piece of legislation of importance regarding Parish Registers is Sir George Rose's Act of 1812 which provided printed form registers for baptisms, marriages and burials that remained the standard form of registration until the introduction of Civil Registration in England and Wales in 1837. As the three principal Church ceremonies continue to the present day, it is of course possible to extend research in the Parish Registers beyond 1837. In fact, as

DEATH

DEATH in the District of   SPRINGSURE   **in the State of Queensland,**

19 23   **Registered by**   Roderick Charles Francis Byrne   District Registrar

Left margin (vertical text): CAUTION—Whosoever shall unlawfully alter any Certified Copy of an Entry in any Register of Births, Marriages, or Deaths, whether by erasure, obliteration, removal, addition, or otherwise, is guilty of a CRIME and liable to the punishment by law provided in that behalf. Vide Sections 486 and 488 of the Criminal Code.

Marginal Notes (if any)	Column		
	1 Number.	872	1441
	Description— 2 When died and where	1st January 1923 Turkey Creek Springsure	
	3 Name and surname; profession, trade, or occupation.	Jeremiah SULLIVAN	Farmer
	4 Sex and age.	Male	94 years
	5 (1) Cause of death.	Senility Heat stroke	
	(2) Duration of last illness.	Heart failure 24 hours	
	(3) Medical attendant by whom certified.	2 hours T.Davies	
	(4) When he last saw deceased.	1st January 1923	
	6 Name and surname of father. Profession, trade, or occupation. Name and maiden surname of mother.	Timothy Sullivan Farmer Mary Callinan	
	7 Signature, description, and residence of informant.	Certified in writing by Denis Sullivan, Son, Glenora, Springsure.	
	8 (1) Signature of Registrar. (2) Date. (3) Place of registration.	R.C.F.Byrne 17th January 1923	Emerald
	If Burial or Cremation Registered— 9 When and where buried or cremated. By whom certified.	2nd January 1923 D.Mitchell	Springsure Cemetery
	10 Name and religion of minister, and/or names of two witnesses of burial or cremation.	J.Bucas John Sullivan	Roman Catholic George Thomson
	11 Where born and how long in Australian States, stating which.	Clonakilty, Cork, Ireland 42 years Queensland	
	If Deceased was Married— 12 (1) Where. (2) At what age. (3) To whom.	Inniskane, Cork, Ireland 36 years Mary Murphy	
	13 Issue living, in order of birth, their names and ages.	Living	years
		Norah	55
		Denis	54
		John	53
		Timothy	52
		Jeremiah	50
		Mary	49
		Patrick	48
		Ellen	46
	Deceased, number and sex.	Deceased	

I,   Harold William Tesch   , Registrar-General, do hereby certify that the above is a true copy of an entry in a Register of Deaths kept in the General Registry Office at Brisbane, and I further certify that I am a person duly authorised by law to issue such certificate.

Extracted on   15 February 1980

Exd. by

Registrar-General

Govt. Printer, Brisbane

ON

The death certificate of Jeremiah Sullivan of Springsure, Queensland, in 1923, forty-two years after he emigrated from Co. Cork, Ireland.

The birth, marriage and death certificates of Sir Winston Churchill, KG show that no differentiation is made for rank in these records, which are common to all citizens of England and Wales, including members of the Royal Family.

French marriage, birth and death certificates. Such certificates can be extremely useful to the family historian because of the amount of information they give. Birth certificates give the hour as well as the date of birth and the dates and places of birth of the parents. Death certificates give the place and date of death, the name of the parents and the widow or widower.

COMMUNE d'UCHIZY
CANTON de TOURNUS
Arrondissement de MACON
Département de SAÔNE-et-LOIRE

RÉPUBLIQUE FRANÇAISE

EXTRAIT
D'ACTE DE MARIAGE

Registre n°
Année 1935
Acte n° 3

Le (1) quinze juin mil neuf cent trente cinq
a été célébré le mariage entre :
(2) Claude Pierre TREMEAU Industriel
né à Chalon sur Saône (Saône et Loire)
le neuf mars mil neuf cent dix
domicilié à 72 Rue du Jeu de Paume à Chalon sur Saône
fils de Louis Emile TREMEAU
et de Marie JAMBON
(3)
et
(4) Marie Joséphine Andrée GUILLOT Sans profession
née à Uchizy (Saône et Loire)
le dix neuf septembre mil neuf cent douze
domiciliée à Uchizy
fille de Jules Charles Marcel GUILLOT "Mort pour la France"
et de Marie Louise Bénédicte GRIVEAUX
(4)
Contrat de mariage reçu par Maître TACHON notaire à Chalon sur Saône
le 1er juin 1935
Mention marginale

Pour extrait conforme
Le 7 novembre 1980
Signature

1. Quantième en chiffres, mois, mois en lettres
2. Nom, prénoms et profession
3. Veuf ou divorcé
4. Idem

COMMUNE d'UCHIZY
CANTON de TOURNUS
Arrondissement de MACON
Département de SAÔNE-et-LOIRE

EXTRAIT
D'ACTE DE NAISSANCE

Registre N°
Année 1943
Folio

Le six mai mil neuf cent quarante trois
à 20 heures 40 en notre commune
est né Monique Jeanne Marie Pierre TREMEAU
du sexe féminin

de Claude Pierre TREMEAU
né le 9 mars 1910
à Chalon sur Saône (Saône et Loire)
(1) et de Marie Joséphine GUILLOT
née le 19 septembre 1912
à Uchizy (Saône et Loire)

Mention marginale : néant — marié — séparé de corps — divorcé — décédé

Inscription au répertoire civil N° 3
Certifié le présent extrait conforme aux indications portées sur le registre par nous
Hippolyte JOSSERAND   officier de l'état civil
de UCHIZY (Saône et loire)
Le 7 novembre 19 80

COMMUNE d'UCHIZY
CANTON de TOURNUS
Arrondissement de MACON
Département de SAÔNE-et-LOIRE

EXTRAIT
D'ACTE DE DÉCÈS

Registre N° R
Année 1965
Folio

Le quatorze octobre mil neuf cent soixante cinq
à 11 heures en la commune de
Chalon sur Saône (Saône et Loire)
est décédée Marie Louise Bénédicte GRIVEAUX

née à LYON 7e (Rhône)
le 2 août 1887
profession sans profession
fille de François Claude GRIVEAUX
et de Marie Floride VILBERT
(1) célibataire époux de ou veuve de Jules Charles Marcel GUILLOT

Certifié le présent extrait conforme aux indications fixées sur le registre par nous
Hippolyte JOSSERAND   officier de l'état civil
de UCHIZY (Saône et Loire)
Le 7 novembre 19 80

· 17 · John Smythe sonne of
John a wakesman

· 17 · James Edardson sonne of
James a taylor

· 17 · Mary Dau sonne daughter of
John a Brokes

20 Elizabeth Dau sonne of
Richard a painters

· 28 · George Euley S of
James a taylor

· 28 · Elizabeth Smyth S of
Thomas a wakesman

6 Thomas a taylor

1523 Anne Euley S of

James a taylor

1523 willm Dobbs sonne of
John a Birdsmurshe

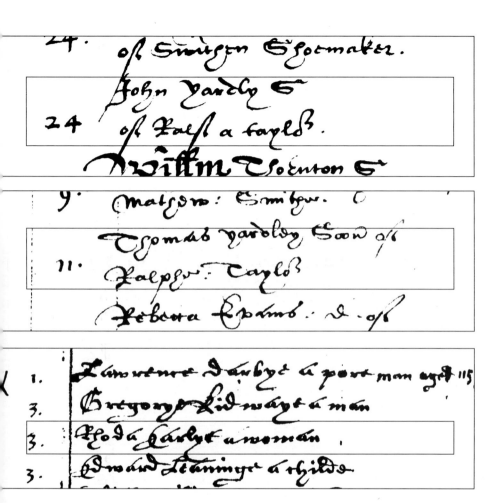

LEFT AND RIGHT
These examples of various spellings of the surname Yardley
found in the register of St Saviour's, Southwark for 1585-1603
show it spelt phonetically as Yearleye, Orley, Erley, Yardley,
Yarly, and Earlye. The George baptised on 28 July 1588 became
Govenor of Virginia as Sir George Yardley.

THE

HOLY BIBLE,

CONTAINING THE

Old and New Teftaments:

Tranflated out of

The Original Tongues:

AND WITH THE

FORMER TRANSLATIONS

Diligently Compared and Revifed,

By His MAJESTY's Special Command.

Appointed to be read in Churches.

O X F O R D,

Printed by *T. Wright* and *W. Gill,* Printers to the U N I V E R S I T Y :
And fold by *S. Crowder,* in Paternofter Row, London ;
and by *W. Jackfon,* in Oxford. 1772.

C U M   P R I V I L E G I O.

and Jews, and this remained the law until the introduction of Civil Registration in 1837. Even then, Nonconformist ministers were not allowed to perform burial rites in parish churchyards until 1880.

A Royal Commission was appointed in 1836 to enquire into the state, custody and authenticity of the 'non-parochial' registers, and to recommend means for their collection and arrangement, legal use and availability. The registers were collected following the Non-Parochial Registers Act of 1836, mainly from most but not all Baptists, Congregationalists, Presbyterians, Methodists, and eventually from the Quakers and some other denominations. The Jews and the majority of Roman Catholics refused to part with their registers which remained in their own custody. The registers were transferred to the Public Record Office in 1961 and comprised 7,000 volumes and files. Before the Quakers surrendered their registers, indexed digests were made. One copy was deposited with the local Quarterly Meeting, and another at the Library of the Society of Friends in London. Also included in this category of records at the Public Record Office are unauthenticated registers of baptisms and marriages performed at the Fleet and Kings Bench Prison, at May Fair and at the Mint at Southwark, which had been deposited in the Bishop of London's Registry in 1821. With one exception – the register of the Independent Church at St Petersburg in Russia – the deposited registers relate solely to England and Wales, but include several registers of Huguenot and other foreign Protestant churches.

In addition there are the headquarters, libraries and museums of various Nonconformist communities which contain extensive records for research (see Appendix III). Enquiries relating to Roman Catholic records should be made to the Archbishop's House in London, or at the local diocesan archives. Jewish records are housed at the Jewish Museum in London and at local synagogues.

Entries relating to Nonconformists often occur in Anglican parish registers; marriages occur as an inevitable consequence of the legislation already mentioned; burials often occur as a practical necessity as many Nonconformists had no burial ground of their own; baptisms are particularly found for the various Methodist

William Currer married Elizabeth Swire March 18th 1777

Alice Currer born May 6th 1778 — babtized & died May 7th 1778

Jennet Currer born March 2nd 1780 — at 20 Min: past 12 in the Morn
babtized April 3rd — Sponsors Mr. Roger Swire
died May 13th 1791. aged 11..2..11   Mrs Currer
                                        Mrs Swire — Proxy for whom Mr —

Elizabeth Currer born March 27th 1782 — 10 Minutes before 7 in the Morn
babtized April 25th — Sponsors The Revd Wm Currer
died Novr 26th 1814. aged 32..8   Jennet Swire
buried at Luddenden 1st Decr 1814   Mrs Higginson her Proxy & Currer

Henry Currer born March 27th 1784 at five in the Morning. Died
babtized May 10th — Sponsors Revd Wm Currer Felby 12th 1817
NB The above Henry Currer laid the Rozer Swire A. 32. 10. buried at
foundation stone of Boy Mill on Friday the Luddenden Felby 17th
18th of Feby 1803 — — — Jno. Currer junr

Elizabeth the Wife of Wm Currer died December 5th 1793 in the
50th year of her Age.

William Currer died Decr 13th 1807 in the 50 year of his
Age — buried at Luddenden on the 17th Decr.

divisions, as they originally saw themselves as members of the Church of England, and not dissenters. Also, for some years after 1696, Anglican clergymen were obliged to record births of Nonconformists.

In recent times various classes of Nonconformist records have come to light and have been deposited at the appropriate county record office, where it is always advisable to make enquiries. Recommended publications are D. J. Steel, *National Index of Parish Registers Vol. II, Sources for Nonconformist Genealogy and Family History* (Society of Genealogists 1973), David Shorney, *Protestant Nonconformity and Roman Catholicism* (PRO 1996) and the *My Ancestors were . . .* series (also published by the Society of Genealogists) with booklets on Quakers, Methodists, Congregationalists, Baptists and English Presbyterian/Unitarians. See also separate chapter entitled 'Huguenot and Jewish Records'.

CATHOLIC RECORDS

The most helpful sources for Catholic genealogy are *The National Index of Parish Registers Vol. III, Sources for Roman Catholic and Jewish Genealogy and Family History* (Society of Genealogists 1974) and a series of booklets published in 1993 by Michael Gandy: *Catholic Parishes in England, Wales and Scotland* and the six-volume *Catholic Missions and Registers (1700–1880)*. The Catholic Family History Society also has very useful publications.

MONUMENTAL INSCRIPTIONS

In many parish churches, monumental inscriptions and tombstones supplement information derived from the registers. Consideration should be given to the parish churchyards, Nonconformist burial grounds and cemeteries authorized by the Act of 1853, which also allowed many cities and boroughs not only to open public cemeteries but also enabled the church and chapel yards to be closed when they were full. There were also private cemeteries which had opened prior to the Act and many more since. Cemetery offices often hold separate registers of cremations which can include useful family data. Some inscriptions have been transcribed and copies are deposited at the Society of Genealogists, the appropriate county record office or library, or the British Library. There is also considerable work being undertaken by local societies to record as much as possible before natural wear and tear, churchyard clearance schemes and vandalism destroy them forever. Registers of local cemeteries are usually kept by the local government authority. If you are able to locate an ancestor's memorial the inscription, including the verse, can contain clues to occupation and career and should be recorded in full and, when practicable, photographed. It is also advisable to look for related burials in the surrounding area as many families wish to be buried close to each other. If it is hard to find out where a burial took place, a search in the British Library, a newspaper library or the county library in local newspapers for obituary notices may help.

THE INTERNATIONAL GENEALOGICAL INDEX

The International Genealogical Index is an index to baptisms and marriages compiled by the Church of Latter-Day Saints, more commonly known as the Mormon Church. The indexes, based mainly on Parish Registers, are arranged alphabetically by county, and while it is neither complete nor wholly accurate it is a useful guide to the original sources. These are available for examination on microfiches and are of the greatest value in establishing the distribution of surnames at any particular period from the sixteenth to nineteenth centuries. A word of warning must, however, be given about the use of the IGI. Much of the information fed into the computer comes from printed or manuscript transcripts of the original registers, and while every effort is made to see that all the entries are accurate, mistakes do occur. For example, when investigating the Bickley family recently it was discovered that many names were listed under the name Buckley. These entries were taken from the parish of St Leonard, Shoreditch, which when the original registers were examined showed clearly how the mistakes had arisen. Furthermore, since only identified infant burials are included in the IGI it may turn out that the individual for whom one is searching and whose name one discovers at about the right time and in the right parish in fact died. This would not show up in the IGI, and one could be led badly astray if one were to rely solely on it. Also some areas are less well covered than others.

The IGI is now also available on CD-ROM, and a search can be made for a name not only in a specific county but also in the whole of a country or a group of countries. The IGI is updated every few years and can be seen at most county record offices (although only that county section may be available) and at LDS Research Centres. It is also available at the Family Records Centre in London as part of the Family Search facility on CD-ROM, which includes LDS Ancestral Files (genealogies submitted to the LDS), the LDS Family History Library Catalogue, indexes to Scottish church records and US Social Security death indexes.

Current indications are that the IGI will be gradually replaced by the new Vital Records Index – the British Isles VRI is now available in CD-ROM format – a new index to births, christenings and marriages, but with as yet very patchy coverage.

OTHER PAROCHIAL RECORDS

Until comparatively recently many social services now undertaken by the State or the local authority were the responsibility of the parishes. It is consequently necessary to take account of how the parish was administered, and the type of records this produced.

The administration of the parish was vested in the clergymen and church wardens, of which there were usually two. Primarily their duties were to ensure that the fabric of the church was maintained, and to administer the property and money for which they were responsible. The records they left are usually called the Vestry Minutes and Churchwardens' Accounts, both of which can contain evidence of value to the family historian as they mention persons to whom payments were made, or from whom money was received for the upkeep of the buildings, purchases of commodities, payment of rates, and other business that will establish informative facts about particular parishioners. In addition, they provide historical material that is of exclusive interest to that particular parish in question.

However, the records of major importance for genealogical research are those of the overseers of the poor. In the sixteenth century, the problem of the poor was acute and vagrancy was widespread due to the dissolution of the monasteries and the increase of enclosures.

By legislation culminating in the Great Poor Law Act of 1601, normally two substantial householders were nominated each year to be Overseers of the Poor, with the duty of maintaining the poor and setting them to work, the funds being provided by parish rates. Further acts required that Houses of Correction should be built for 'rogues, vagrants, lewd women who have bastards, and parents leaving their children chargeable to the parish who shall be brought before the justices for committal'.

Later legislation established the law of settlement and removal which contained the provision that any strangers settling in a parish might be removed by the justices unless they rented a tenement of not less than £10 annual value or found security to discharge the parish of their adoption from all expenses that may be incurred upon their behalf, or they brought a 'settlement certificate' from their own parish accepting liability for any charges. The Act also authorized the justices to transport to the plantations in the colonies incorrigible rogues, vagabonds and sturdy beggars. Further legislation provided that serving a parish office, paying a parish rate, residing in the parish, being bound apprentice by indenture to a parishioner, or, if unmarried, serving a year in the service of the parish, established settlement.

There was also concern about the prevention of vagrancy, and in 1743/4 a reward of 5s. was introduced for the apprehension of any vagrant and removal, after whipping or confinement, to their place of settlement. Incorrigible rogues were treated more harshly. After six months' imprisonment, with whipping at the justices' discretion, they were either sent home or impressed into naval or military service. Persons sheltering vagabonds were fined a sum of from 10s. to 40s. Vagrants' children could be apprenticed by the justices, and bastard children of vagrant women were not to gain a settlement in the parish of their birth. They were in fact hastened from one parish to another to make sure that the baby was born under someone else's haystack. This treatment caused a scandal, as a high proportion of mothers and babies died as a result of this policy.

Throughout the eighteenth century there was considerable litigation between parishes. A parish would claim that someone was settled elsewhere; the individual concerned would then be examined before a justice, reciting his life history in a document of fascinating detail; his legal place of settlement would be determined and he would be sent there; if the receiving parish had doubts about the legal settlement, a re-examination would be ordered. All efforts were concentrated on avoiding one's own parish having to pay relief. The consequent proceedings, of course, are of great genealogical value.

In 1781/2, because of the 'incapacity, negligence or misconduct' of Overseers, and the 'sufferings and distresses of the poor being most grievous', provisions were made for the inspection of workhouses, and no poor were to be sent into a workhouse more than ten miles from their own parish, also no persons except the indigent were to be sent to the workhouse, and no children under the age of seven years were to be forcibly separated from their parents.

A further act in 1792 dealt with the abuses of the removal of vagrants. In future, no reward was to be paid for their apprehension until they had been punished, and no female vagrant was to be whipped for any reason whatsoever. In 1794/5 no person was to be removed until they were actually chargeable, and the justices were authorized to suspend at their discretion orders of removal upon sick and infirm people. It was also in 1795 that the meeting of Berkshire justices at the George and Pelican Inn at Speenhamland took place. This gave its name to the ill-advised Speenhamland System under which a scale of relief, based on the size of the family and the price of bread, was devised. It never received statutory recognition, but the example was followed throughout the country, and tables showing the 'Speenhamland Act of Parliament' were displayed in ale houses for the edification of their clientele.

Following a Royal Commission of Inquiry, which reported scathingly on the whole system of parochial poor relief, the Poor Law Reform Act of 1834 was passed. Under this act, the responsibility was transferred from individual parishes to groups of them in Poor Law Unions. The major events in the subsequent history of the Poor Law were the transfer of its administration from the unions to the county councils in 1929, and, finally, the assumption by the central government in 1948 and 1966 of responsibility, not only for the broad lines of 'public assistance' and 'social security', but also for much the greater part of its detailed administration.

It may come as a surprise to learn that in the sixteenth century the birth of illegitimate children seems to have been an unusual event. Such an occurrence was becoming more common in the seventeenth century, and so common as to create little surprise from about 1750 onwards.

The concern shown in this matter by the parish was not solely a moral one, as there was also the more material problem of maintenance on the parish rates. Therefore, if the father could be identified, he was made responsible for the maintenance of the child. If, therefore, the Parish Register only gives the mother's name, a record of the father's may be found elsewhere among parochial records.

Most poor children were bound apprentices at an early age. By the eighteenth century the old rules governing apprenticeships were disappearing, and they were often used as a convenient way of providing for a pauper child. Most were indentured to learn husbandry or housewifery in their own parish, and this usually resulted in them being used as agricultural labourers or female servants. Those apprenticed elsewhere were indentured to a variety of trades, rarely skilled ones. However, there were abuses of pauper apprenticeship. For the worst, one must consult the records of the mills in manufacturing towns and villages which imported pauper children by the wagon-load from London, contracting to take 'one idiot in every twenty', where the conditions were indescribably horrible, and where the graveyards hold scores of the small bodies of these unfortunates who were literally worked to death.

The Parish Constable was chosen annually from the residents of the parish, and men usually served in rotation. The Constable was appointed by the Justices of the Peace of the county, and was responsible for maintaining law and order, caring for the stocks and whipping post; the apprehension of rogues, vagabonds and others, and bringing them before the magistrates; the arrest of those ordered to appear in court; administering punishments to convicted offenders; accompanying vagrants and others to the House of Correction; and various other relevant duties as required. By 1856 the office of Parish Constable had been superseded by the county and town Police Force or Constabulary. The records of the constables throw much light on the activities of parishioners.

Overseers of the Highways, or Waywardens, looked after the roads and bridges in the parish. They had to pay for the upkeep of roads, which resulted in taxes being levied in the parish. The accounts of the Overseers, where they survive, show who owned property and paid taxes, and also show payments to contractors and individuals who did the work required, and are therefore useful as background material.

The Parish Clerk kept the minutes of the Vestry Meetings, cared for the parish registers and Banns Book, and sometimes led the singing in church. Other duties may have included being the sexton (grave-digger) and caretaker of the church and churchyard. The Sexton's Book, if available, gives details of burials, and often contains far more information than the burial entries in the parish register.

Each county and borough had its Court of Quarter Sessions, and it not only dealt with criminal cases, but also performed the duties of local government before county councils existed. Typical of such matters are those ensuring that the major highways were kept in good repair; paying coroners for their inquisitions; committing vagrants and others to the House of Correction; committal and release of debtors from gaol; payment for burial of those who died whilst passing through the county; inspection of workhouses and, if warranted, bringing the parish officers to court for orders to be made against them; bodysnatching cases; poaching; and instructions and orders to the parish constables.

Finally there are the charity records. Charities of early medieval foundation still exist, and in early times they were almost invariably entrusted for administration to the parish clergymen and church-wardens. Some typical charities concerned themselves with food, education, loans, clothing, skilled apprenticeships for poor children, and coal and fuel.

In all the parish records we have mentioned it is almost certain that somewhere you will find a mention of your ancestors, no matter what their status within the community. Apart from providing valuable evidence of their existence, these records give a fascinating insight into the type of persons they were, and create a picture of the environment in which they lived.

The great majority of these records are now deposited at county record offices and it is always there that you should first enquire.

8

DATING

The generally known basic fact, and for many purposes all that need be considered, is that before 1752 the official English calendar reckoned the year as beginning on 25 March ('old style' or O.S.) and from 1752 the year was reckoned from 1 January ('new style' or N.S.), and that it is customary to show the year by double indication for dates between 1 January and 24 March; thus for example 24 March 1715 should be written 24 March 1715/16, and the following day would be 25 March 1716. The double indication can be found in some registers before 1752.

This much is quite well known, but there were complications which affect church registers. The fact that both were changed in one year by the New Style Calendar Act has obscured the point that there were two quite separate factors involved: (a) the 25 March new year was English practice from the twelfth century until 1751; (b) England used until 1752 the Julian calendar which incorporated a miscalculation of leap years; this had been amended by Pope Gregory XIII to produce the Gregorian calendar in 1582; this was promptly adopted in Catholic countries, but, as a 'popish invention', less readily so by Protestant countries. Most of Europe had been using the 1 January new year before 1582. The New Style Calendar Act made two changes in the official calendar: (a) with effect from 1 January 1752, the calendar year was reckoned from 1 January and (b) eleven days, 3–13 September 1752, were omitted to adjust to the Gregorian calendar, with adjusted calculation of leap years thereafter.

The English colonies including North America used the official English calendar; Scotland, however, adopted a 1 January new year in 1600, although retaining the Julian calendar; Britain and its colonies were, therefore, ten days (1582–1699) or eleven days (1700–52) out of phase with the calendar used in much of Western Europe.

In the first place, and although surprisingly the fact seems to have failed to be noticed in any standard reference sources, it seems to have been quite widespread practice for a 1 January calendar year to have been used in earlier sixteenth century registers. A few examples survive, but it seems that many registers were altered to a 25 March year when they were transcribed onto parchment in about 1600; the registers of Chudleigh, Devon, and Fareham, Hampshire, show that the transcribers got into a muddle when changing the dates. Some modern transcribers of registers have also adjusted the dating of their work to a 1 January year basis, rather than preserving the text of the original document, which can cause confusion.

The earlier Presbyterians also had a tendency to use a 1 January new year basis before 1752; for example Tavistock Abbey Chapel registers record in 1693 'N.B. the year is supposed to begin from that we commonly call New Year's Day' and date the records accordingly. This may be in part attributable to a significant number of ministers with Scottish names, presumably used to the Scottish calendar. Similar tendencies can be found among denominations with continental European links; Catholics, Huguenots and Moravians in particular. (One register of a Moravian congregation in London goes so far as to date entries before 1752 by both the Julian and Gregorian calendars.)

The Society of Friends used official English reckoning for the year but objected to months and days of the week named after heathen gods. They used a numerical system, Sunday being 'first-day' and Saturday 'seventh-day'; months before 1752 were March, 'first month' round to February, 'twelfth month'; thus the calendar year started on the 25th of the first month. (The months September to December, being Latin numeration concurring with Friends' numeration, were acceptable.) From 1752, this was changed, January being 'first month' and December 'twelfth month', and this was specified by a printed notice circulated in September 1751 to all meetings in Great Britain, Ireland and America, from the London Meeting for Sufferings.

The Jewish calendar is an extremely complicated subject, outside the scope of this book beyond stating that the Jewish epoch dates (by Christian reckoning) from 1 October 3761BC, and the year varies between 353 and 385 days in twelve or thirteen months. A detailed account can be found in the *Encyclopaedia Judaica*.

REGNAL YEARS

Many official documents and wills refer to dates in terms of the year of the reign of the sovereign in question, e.g. 26 June 13 Chas II (26 June 1661). The regnal year dates from the first day of the reign of each sovereign, thus the first year of Queen Elizabeth I began on 17 November 1558, the date of her accession, and lasted until 16 November 1559.

The following is a list of the regnal years of the kings and queens since the Norman Conquest.

William I	14 Oct 1066 to 9 Sep 1087
William II	9 Sep 1087 to 1 Aug 1100
Henry I	1 Aug 1100 to 2 Dec 1135
Stephen 2	Dec 1135 to 25 Oct 1154
Henry II	25 Oct 1154 to 13 Aug 1189
Richard I	13 Aug 1189 to 6 Apr 1199
John	6 Apr 1199 to 17 Oct 1216
Henry III	17 Oct 1216 to 16 Nov 1272
Edward I	16 Nov 1272 to 8 Jul 1307
Edward II	8 Jul 1307 to 25 Jan 1326/7
Edward III	25 Jan 1326/7 to 22 Jun 1377

Richard II	22 Jun 1377 to 30 Sep 1399
Henry IV	30 Sep 1399 to 21 Mar 1412/13
Henry V	21 Mar 1412/13 to 1 Sep 1422
Henry VI	1 Sep 1422 to 4 Mar 1460/1
Edward IV	4 Mar 1460/1 to 9 Apr 1483
Edward V	9 Apr 1483 to 22 Jun 1483
Richard III	22 Jun 1483 to 22 Aug 1485
Henry VII	22 Aug 1485 to 22 Apr 1509
Henry VIII	22 Apr 1509 to 28 Jan 1546/7
Edward VI	28 Jan 1546/7 to 6 Jul 1553
Mary I and Philip	6 Jul 1553 to 17 Nov 1558
Elizabeth I	17 Nov 1558 to 24 Mar 1602/3
James I	24 Mar 1602/3 to 27 Mar 1625/6
Charles I	27 Mar 1625/6 to 30 Jan 1648/9

(*Note*: The assumption is that there is a complete continuity of the Crown, and therefore the throne is never vacant. Despite the interregnum, Charles II ascended the throne upon the death of Charles I and remained in exile until 1660. Dates during the interregnum are usually given in *anno Domini*.)

Charles II	30 Jan 1648/9 to 6 Feb 1684/5
James II	6 Feb 1684/5 to 13 Feb 1688/9
William III and Mary II	13 Feb 1688/9 to 28 Dec 1694
William III alone	13 Feb 1694/5 to 8 Mar 1701/2
Anne	8 Mar 1701/2 to 1 Aug 1714
George I	1 Aug 1714 to 11 Jun 1727
George II	11 Jun 1727 to 25 Oct 1760
George III	25 Oct 1760 to 29 Jan 1820
George IV	29 Jan 1820 to 26 Jun 1830
William IV	26 Jun 1830 to 20 Jun 1837
Victoria	20 Jun 1837 to 22 Jan 1901

From the beginning of the reign of Queen Victoria, a knowledge of the regnal years is not of any importance for genealogical purposes, since all documents were dated *anno Domini*.

9

CELTIC ANCESTORS

The inhabitants of Cornwall and Wales, as well as of Scotland and Ireland, were Celtic rather than Anglo-Saxon. As in the early 1800s half the population of the British Isles lived in these areas it is an important aspect, and family history in these areas has some particular features as a result of the racial background. The first is surnames: all of the Celtic races originally used 'patronymics' rather than surnames, which means that in place of a surname they used their father's and/or their grandfather's christian names.

So, for example, a Welshman called 'Evan ap Llewellyn ap Owen' was Evan son of Llewellyn, son of Owen, and Cornishmen would use the same formula, but without the 'ap', so a Cornishman named John Richard William was John son of Richard son of William. In the course of time these became fixed as regular surnames – generally earlier at higher social levels and in the less remote areas, and later among poorer people and in remoter areas. So a squire in Monmouthshire or East Cornwall would have adopted a fixed surname before 1600, but a labourer near Lands End or in Snowdonia could be found using a patronymic name in the 1750s. Mostly these became fixed as surnames simply as Williams, Jones (John), etc. But some Welsh names slurred the 'ap' so that 'ap Richard' became 'Prichard', and similarly Prees or Price, Proger, Bowen and Bevan derive from ap Rhys, ap Roger, ap Owen and ap Evan.

In Scotland and Ireland it worked similarly but the Gaelic language gave them 'Mac' for 'son of' and (only in Ireland) 'Ui, or 'O' for 'grandson of', and so you get the numerous names beginning in 'Mac' and 'O'. But these were further complicated by the clan system so that not only would everyone descending from the original Donald call themselves MacDonald, but others who joined the clan would as well, although not related. The Scots tended to keep their prefix 'Mac', but quite often the Irish have dropped the 'O' in more recent years. For example, President Ronald Reagan's great-grandfather in County Tipperary began his life as Michael O'Regan. The Scots and the Irish began using fixed surnames earlier than the Welsh or Cornish.

As well as the clan system, genealogy was important to the Celts for inheritance of their land. Welshmen, for example, inherited land by 'gavelkind', equal shares for each child, and so preserved their genealogies as title deeds to their lands. For many people, from kings to abbots and minor chieftains, their position depended upon their kinship as much as it did for small farmers. As a result there is a great deal of genealogy preserved from very early dates; the O'Neills of Ulster have the most ancient documented pedigree in Western Europe, and there is the saying 'as long as a Welsh pedigree'.

Nor should it be thought that these ancient pedigrees are out of reach of ordinary people. A minor Scottish customs official has been traced back to Ailill Olum, King of Munster in Ireland, one and a half millennia before, and President Ronald Reagan is a great-great-grandson of Thomas O'Regan, a poor landless labourer who none the less descends from Raigan, nephew of the great King Brian Boru, a thousand years before.

But all too often, Celtic genealogy gets lost in the confusion of too many people with a single surname, with inadequate records to distinguish who is who; Jones and Davies in Wales, Williams and Thomas in Cornwall, MacDonald and Campbell in Scotland,

Murphy and O'Brien in Ireland. There is a glen in the Scottish Highlands where every family was surnamed Ross, and 132 Ryan families in a single village in Tipperary. Add to this the problem, all too often, of laxity in keeping more recent records, and the common problem of Celtic genealogy is to bridge the gap between nineteenth- and twentieth-century records and the earlier traditional pedigrees.

Some of the paucity of records is due to causes like the Hebrideans, who kept no parish registers as, firstly, everyone knew everyone's family history anyway, so why write it down? and secondly, few if any of them could read or write. Oral family history is important, for many old people can remember traditions of families, often surprisingly far back. One man's grandmothers, one Irish, one Scottish, gave him a great deal of the story of his ancestors, and the intense interest that Celts have in their own and their neighbours' ancestors is surprising until you remember it is a habit ingrained for a thousand years and more.

It is important to remember that the Celts had their own languages: Irish and Scottish Gaelic, Welsh and (now extinct) Cornish. Only the earlier records are written in these languages, but a trap is when surnames are anglicized, for example when the Scottish or Irish 'Gowan' and Cornish 'Gof' get translated as Smith.

WALES

Apart from the aspects discussed above, the more recent Welsh records are organized in the English way, as described in earlier chapters. The archives are divided between the National Library of Wales at Aberystwyth, and the local county record offices. The National Library remains the key source, and also holds a treasurehouse of ancient Welsh genealogies.

SCOTLAND

In Scotland, the archives are ideally organized. The parish registers of the (Presbyterian) Church of Scotland were all called in to the central archives in 1855, and this coincides with the start of Scottish General Registration on 1 January 1855. Moreover, in recent years the Church of Jesus Christ of Latter-Day Saints were permitted to microfilm all Old Parish Registers, as they are known in Scotland, and copies of the resulting microfilm are available not only in New Register House in Edinburgh but also in the LDS Church libraries. Moreover, the microfilmed copies of births/baptisms and marriages have been computer-indexed; the index can also be consulted at the Family Records Centre in London, where the 'Scottish Link' facility also provides access, for an hourly fee, to Scottish civil registration records; these are also available via family history centres. There are also census records open to the public up to 1891.

Nearly all the Scottish archives a family historian will need are sited very conveniently near each other in Edinburgh. New Register House, in Princes Street, holds records of births, marriages and deaths, parish registers, census returns, some army, navy and air force registers and other miscellaneous records. Other sources are held in the adjacent Scottish Record Office or its branch repository, West Register House, in Charlotte Square. In addition to the usual sources of General Registration, parish registers, wills (called 'testaments' in Scotland) and census records, there is a further vast series of records unique in Europe, which reflect the fact that the Law of Scotland is based upon Roman Law rather than upon the Common Law of England, Ireland and America. These records are legal ones, relating particularly to the ownership, inheritance and acquisition of land, of which the most important are 'Services of Heirs' and 'Sasines'. Since in Scotland land could not be devised by a will but could only pass by either inheritance or by legal act, a great deal of the genealogy of any owners of land and their relations is recorded in these archives. In general the wealth of material available in Edinburgh means that researching Scottish family history should be a happy task.

IRELAND

Irish research is a subject on its own, but an important one, as in 1801 one-third of the population of the British Isles lived in Ireland. To understand Irish research one needs to understand Irish history. The truly Irish people have ancient roots in their country, and this is the race to whom much of Europe is indebted for a legacy of Christianity and culture.

In the Middle Ages, Anglo-Norman knights invaded Ireland and became assimilated – 'more Irish than the Irish themselves'. Burke, for example, is the Norman name de Burgo. Later settlers in Ireland were Protestant, as distinct from the ancient race which was, and has mostly remained, Roman Catholic. From England came the so-called 'Anglo-Irish' landowners, merchants, and the like; from Scotland came Presbyterians who largely settled in the northern Irish province of Ulster – these being usually termed in America the 'Scotch-Irish'. There were other much smaller groups too, such as the Huguenots from France and the Palatines from Germany. In the later seventeenth and for much of the eighteenth centuries, penal laws repressed the Catholics, and most power and wealth was represented by the 'Protestant Ascendancy' of the Anglo-Irish. As a result, early Catholic church registers are rare, and they left few other records as they could not, for example, legally own land.

The difficulties of Irish research tend to be exaggerated, because the Public Record Office at the Four Courts in Dublin was burnt down in 1922, and much of what was there was lost. However, it has to be appreciated that only about half the existing Church of Ireland (Protestant Episcopal) parish registers were lost in the fire – and the majority of those were from small rural parishes with few Protestant inhabitants, while seven-eighths of the population were Catholic or Presbyterian, whose parish registers were not in the record office in 1922, and so were not lost. Certainly the original probate court records were also lost, but a great many of these wills survive as copies or in the abstracts. The general question of Irish research is governed by the scattered nature of the records, which is in many ways a blessing as this saved them from loss in 1922.

Northern Ireland, six counties in the province of Ulster, became separate in 1922, and many local records are held there, but as Dublin was the capital of all of Ireland until that date, some important archives relating to the North are still in Dublin. For example, one such treasury of information is at the Registry of Deeds at King's Inn in Dublin where all property deeds and records such as wills relating to property are recorded (much like an American county courthouse, but with all thirty-two counties recorded together) after 1708, and at the Genealogical Office in

Dublin there are the recorded pedigrees of many of the Anglo-Irish landowners and their families.

General Registration of births, marriages and deaths in Ireland began on 1 January 1864 (although registration of Protestant marriages began in 1845) and copies of the Dublin registrations relating to the Northern six counties are held in Belfast. Parish registers of all denominations for the six counties, or microfilms of them, are also either held in the Public Record Office of Northern Ireland, Belfast, or are being gathered in.

In the twenty-six counties of the South, the Republic of Ireland, records of General Registration are kept at the General Register Office, Dublin. For parish registers it is much more complicated: Catholic registers (which relate to the great majority of the population) are held by the individual parish priests, but microfilms of all of these prior to 1880 are at the National Library in Dublin – although the written permission of the respective bishop is sometimes necessary before they can be examined. Church of Ireland registers are largely still held by the rectors of each parish, although increasingly the registers, or copies or microfilms of them, are being deposited at the National Archives in Dublin. Quaker records are kept at the Library of the Society of Friends, Donnybrook, Dublin. Other important archives in Dublin are held by Trinity College, the Representative Body of the Church of Ireland, and for lawyers, the Library at King's Inn. The period before the suppression of native Irish culture in the seventeenth century is superbly documented in the library of the Royal Irish Academy. Finally, it should be remembered that all of Ireland was governed from London before 1922, and many records are in British archives (particularly of the Army, Navy and police).

Census returns were another casualty, but Griffith's *Valuation of Ireland* (1848–64), which is now available as a CD-ROM, goes some way towards compensating for this loss: this was a survey of land tenure whose purpose was to establish a way of raising poor relief. There is a surname index to Griffith's *Valuation* and the *Tithe Applotment Books* (*ca* 1823–38), created by the National Library and known as the Index of Surnames or Householders' Index.

In recent years local heritage centres have been established throughout Ireland, some of which offer a research service. A comprehensive guide to Irish research can be found in John Grenham's *Tracing your Irish Ancestors* (1992).

In essence, Irish research is not easy, but the difficulties are often exaggerated, and a great deal can be accomplished with care and application. The reward for success can be connection with some of the oldest documented pedigrees in Western Europe.

10

HUGUENOT AND
JEWISH RECORDS

Throughout history the British Isles have played host to people from all over Europe, and more recently from all over the world, who wished to settle here. There are many Britons whose parents or grandparents came here as refugees from tyrannical regimes in Europe, the chief of these being Jews, Poles and Russians.

During the eighteenth and nineteenth centuries a few permanent refugees came to Britain, fleeing the French Revolution, and Germans came in the wake of the Hanoverian Kings. From the family historian's point of view one of the largest groups of immigrants were the Huguenots who came in large numbers during the sixteenth and seventeenth centuries, and it is with them that we propose to concern ourselves in this chapter.

The origins of French Protestantism are to be found in the teachings of Erasmus and Luther. As elsewhere in northern Europe it was the availability of printed bibles almost more than anything else which had such a profound effect on the academic, professional and artisan classes of society. The Church reacted vigorously and the faculty of theology of the Sorbonne obtained from François I an ordinance in 1535 for the suppression of printing. However the demand for bibles grew rapidly, and wherever they were read in the vernacular, the movement for reform grew apace.

The Huguenots had been assured that liberty of conscience would be granted, and showed themselves to be loyal subjects on the accession of Louis XIV, when their rights under the Edict of Nantes were reaffirmed. Once Louis XIV gained his majority, persecution began to increase and rights offered by the Edict of Nantes were eroded until its final revocation in 1685. More than 400 proclamations, edicts and declarations attacking the Huguenots in their households, civil freedom, property and liberty of conscience were promulgated between 1660 and 1685, in the course of which time more than 200,000 Huguenots left France to seek sanctuary in Switzerland, Germany, the Netherlands and England.

Owing to the restrictions placed upon their movements by these Edicts, those from south-east France mainly went to Switzerland, seeking the shortest route. Those in the north-east and some from the north-west went to the Netherlands; most from the north-west and south-west came to England. From Normandy, Picardy and the Pas de Calais they arrived in strength in Kent and Sussex. Those using the Atlantic route from Saintonge and Aunis formed the basis of the French churches in the west of England. However, it did not mean that all would stay at their first port of refuge. Those who eventually settled in Germany travelled via Switzerland, and the American Huguenots mainly descend from those who had at first sought refuge in England. During the last decade of the seventeenth century, when William of Orange was not only Stadtholder of the Netherlands but also King of the United Kingdom, there was a great interchange of refugees between the Netherlands, England and Ireland.

It is always natural that refugees should choose to live near their fellow countrymen, especially where communities exist that have been established as a result of previous migration. Such places in England were London and Canterbury. Some emigrants were close to and used the liturgy of the Church of England, but others were closer to Presbyterian doctrines and were classed as Nonconformists. Between 1681 and 1720 approximately 200,000 Huguenots left

France and of these it is thought that some 40,000 came to England and of those, about 15,000 settled in London. This migration, spread over forty years, should be seen in the context of the contemporary population of London in 1700, which was 50,000.

The Huguenots settled in two main London colonies, in Soho and Spitalfields. Spitalfields already had a long tradition of political and religious disaffection, and was a stronghold of nonconformity. The silk weaving industry had already been established there in the first half of the century, so it was a natural rallying point for immigrant Huguenot artisans, particularly those skilled in that industry.

Why Soho became the other great centre is not so clear. It was possibly because the French congregation had settled in that part of Westminster in the 1640s. In 1682, when large scale migration from France began, these refugees were granted a lease of the Greek Chapel in Soho, which no doubt attracted many of them to this quarter of London. It also seems that many who settled in Soho were of bourgeois and aristocratic backgrounds. This is supported by the fact that many of these refugees were goldsmiths or silversmiths, jewellers, engravers, clock and watchmakers, or tapestry weavers, who naturally gravitated to the fashionable residential quarter of London near to the Court.

By the second half of the eighteenth century the specifically Huguenot character of both Soho and Spitalfields had declined greatly. Many of the refugee families had become anglicized through intermarriage and knew nothing of the persecution which had originally brought them from Europe. By 1800 only two Huguenot chapels survived in Soho, but one chapel in Spitalfields was still using the French language in 1840. During this period, the centre of the silk weaving industry moved from Spitalfields to Bethnal Green and this no doubt helped to destroy many of the French influences and ways of life which had been prevalent in Spitalfields. But there remains a French church in Soho Square to this day.

Huguenot records in France vary according to locality. In the country as a whole there are few which begin before 1660, but those of Caen, La Rochelle, Rouen and Nîmes are very extensive and begin at the end of the sixteenth century and continue up to the Revocation of the Edict of Nantes in 1685. The usefulness of French Protestant records is not confined to English and American families of Huguenot descent. They contain many references to English, Scottish and Irish Protestant families resident in France, and especially to merchants trading between British and French ports.

For those who have Huguenot ancestors, membership of the Huguenot Society is of great value. The society's transactions include transcriptions of all Huguenot parish registers as well as naturalization papers and kindred material. Three books published in 1985, the tercentenary of the Revocation of the Edict of Nantes, are of exceptional importance to those of Huguenot descent. They are *Huguenot Heritage* by Robin Gwynn; *A Family from Flanders* by John Peters; and *Huguenot Ancestry* by Noel Currer-Briggs and Royston Gambier.

The medieval Jewish communities in England (Jews were prominent in Exeter) were expelled in 1290. Small crypto-Jewish communities existed in London and Bristol in the sixteenth century, but due to contemporary persecution they were outwardly Christian and were recorded in Anglican registers. The official readmission of Jews dates from 1655, the earliest being Sephardim from Portugal and Spain who settled in London. Later arrivals were Ashkenazim from Germany and Central Europe (some coming via the British colonies in the West Indies and North America) and it is these who are relevant outside London. The oldest surviving Ashkenazi synagogue in the country is that at Plymouth founded in 1768. Their activities were in specialized trades, for example as jewellers or tailors, or in naval victualling, and international commerce. Jews suffered numerous legal disabilities until the nineteenth century, only being allowed to own property from 1728, have British nationality from 1740, vote in elections from 1835, and graduate at universities from 1870. However, their religion did not bar their wills from the Christian Church probate courts.

Jewish records are a specialized subject on their own. Firstly, certain of them are in Hebrew or Yiddish, some using the Hebrew alphabet and the Jewish calendar. Secondly, what is recorded is largely distinct from Christian registers; for example birth records are rare, and commonly there are only registers of circumcision of boys (at eight days old); conversely marriage records are particularly good, often including the marriage contract, despite Jewish marriages being exempted from Lord Hardwicke's Marriage Act of 1754; surnames are a particular difficulty, as these were often changed, and secular surnames may not occur in synagogue records where the patronymic (for example Moses ben Jacob) was used. Wills are a particularly valuable source, and due to a good deal of mobility a large proportion were proved in the Prerogative Court of Canterbury, but many other sources are eliminated by legal disabilities; for example Jews did not have a vote before 1835 so they do not appear in earlier voters lists or poll books.

There are extensive collections of material (including many researched pedigrees) at the Jewish Museum, London, and the Mocatta Library, University College, London. The Wiener Library, holding a great deal of German and other continental material (relevant in so far as nearly all British Jews are of immigrant origin) has been transferred to Tel Aviv. Recommended publications are Isobel Mordy, *My Ancestors were Jewish* (Society of Genealogists 1995); the *National Index of Parish Registers Vol. III, Sources for Roman Catholic and Jewish Genealogy and Family History* (Society of Genealogists 1974); and Cecil Roth, *The Rise of Provincial Jewry* (1950). Since most Jews in England are of immigrant origins, the extensive material on aliens at the Public Record Office, Kew, particularly in classes HO 1 to HO 4, is invaluable.

11

WILLS,
ADMINISTRATIONS
AND INVENTORIES

<><>

Wills and their associated documents are a particularly important record for the family historian. Often they are the only truly personal document a person has left, and the only clue we have to them as people rather than names on a piece of paper or parchment. But, as you will see, they are a complicated subject.

1858 ONWARDS
Since January 1858 wills in England and Wales have been proved centrally at the Principal Probate Registry which was until recently at Somerset House in London, and in Ireland at the Principal Probate Registries in Dublin, and, since 1922, Belfast. The law governing wills in Scotland is different from that in the rest of Britain; testamentary matters in the Channel Islands and in the Isle of Man are still in the jurisdiction of the local courts. Annual indexes of Grants of Probate and Letters of Administration in England and Wales can be consulted at the Principal Registry (First Avenue House, High Holborn, London WC1V 6NP) and at most county record offices. Copies of wills and administrations may be

obtained from the Principal Registry for a fee.

Before the establishment of the Principal Probate Registry in 1858 the probate of any will in England and Wales took place in one of at least three hundred courts depending upon the location of the estate of the deceased. There was a hierarchy of Church courts; at the head were the Archbishops' Prerogative Courts of Canterbury and York (PCC and PCY) and the local courts of the Bishops and Archdeacons. There were also areas of 'Peculiar or exempt jurisdiction of Church and other dignitaries' which did not come under the Bishops or Archdeacons' Courts at all.

Probate records of the land-owning classes and the wealthy are most likely to be found in PCC, at the Public Record Office – for which there are comprehensive indexes up to 1800; the records can be seen at the Family Records Centre in London. The Prerogative Court of York, of which the records are at the Borthwick Institute at York, filled the same role for the northern province (Cheshire, Cumberland, Durham, Lancashire, Northumberland, Nottinghamshire, Westmorland and Yorkshire). Their records were not solely confined to the wealthy, and the indexes and calendars should always be searched in addition to those of local courts.

Details of the exact jurisdiction of each court, the location of their records, and the existence of printed and other indexes, are given in two books: *Wills and their Whereabouts*, by Anthony J. Camp (1974), gives full details of all types of probate records in each diocesan and other record office, and describes the probate procedure fully; *Probate Jurisdictions: Where to Look for Wills* by J. S. W. Gibson (4th ed. 1994, Federation of Family History Societies) is clearly arranged by (historic) county, with maps to show jurisdictions, and is designed specifically for the inexperienced; either will set the searcher for probate records on the right path. These two books also give details of probate records in Scotland, Ireland, and in the Channel Islands and for the Isle of Man (for which probate matters are still dealt with locally). Many testators elsewhere in the British Isles also had property in England and Wales, so their wills also may appear in PCC.

Properly speaking, a 'will' deals with real estate, though under Scottish law before 1868 and certain Channel Islands law only personal (i.e. movable) property could be bequeathed. A 'testament' deals with the bequest of personal goods such as clothing, furniture, stock, farming implements, trade tools, bonds, book debts or money in any form; hence the phrase 'last will and testament'. In cases of intestacy or where there was a defect in the will the next of kin or a creditor applied for letters of administration. The Administration Act was entered in a book and there was also the Administration Bond whereby the administrator gave security for acting properly. It was usual to submit an inventory of the deceased's goods with the will, and almost invariably with administrations, especially before about 1720. Inventories are sometimes found filed with wills and sometimes separately, as in the case of wills and administrations proved in the Prerogative Court of Canterbury, and as they list the deceased's possessions, are a fascinating record for a family historian.

Much of the text of a will is of less relevance to genealogists and so the text can often be summarized. It was customary, for example, to start the will with the set-piece declaration of faith; for example,

In the name of God, Amen. The sixth day of December in the year of our Lord God one thousand six hundred fifty and fower I, William Currer of Middleton in the parish of Ilkley and county of Yorke, yeoman sick of body but of perfect memory (praysed be God for it) doe ordaine and make this my last will and testament in manner and forme following: First I commend my soule into the hands of Almighty God my Creator who gave it trustinge by the onlie merritts and mediacion of his sonne and blessed Saviour Jesus Christ . . . And my body to the earthe to be buried in the parish church of Ilkley aforesayd at the stall-head where I had my seat formerly at the discretion of my friends And for my worldly goods that God hath beene pleased to bestow upon mee my will and mynde is that they shalbe to 'such and such uses' as hereafter shalbe expressed.

The whole of this lengthy preamble and committal can be summarized as follows: 'William Currer of Middleton, Ilkley, Yorks, yeoman. Will made 6 December 1654. To be buried in the parish church of Ilkley. Usual committal.' The will continues as follows:

Item I give unto Dorothy my wife the third part as the law doth require of all the remainder of my goods.

Item I give unto my sonne Henry Currer twenty pounds as a legacie to be paid within one year next after my decease to be put forth for his use.

Item I give unto my five children Henry Currer my sayd sonne Alice Currer, Jane Currer, Mary Currer and Anne Currer my daughters.

and so on in greater or less complexity, and often including long complicated legal provisions governing the descent of property and the management of the estates of children who were under age. This particular will ends thus:

Item I make Dorothy Currer my sayd wife and Henry my aforesayd sonne sole executors of this my last will and testament Sealed with my seale and signed the day and yeare above written: William Currer. Sealed and signed in the sight and presence of us Thomas Ferrand Agnes Ferrand Thomas Guyland.

At the end of the will there will be the probate act, in this case in English because the will was made during the Commonwealth, when, from 1653 to 1660, all wills were proved centrally in London at the Family Records Centre. Usually the probate is in Latin, but the form is very much the same, except that the name of the ecclesiastical court is given.

This will was proved at London the sixth day of February in the year of our Lord God according to the computation of the Church of England one thousand six hundred fifty and five before the Judges for probate of wills and granting administrations lawfully authorized by the oathes of Dorothy Currer the relict and Henry Currer the naturall and lawfull sonne of the sayd deceased joynt executors named in this last will and

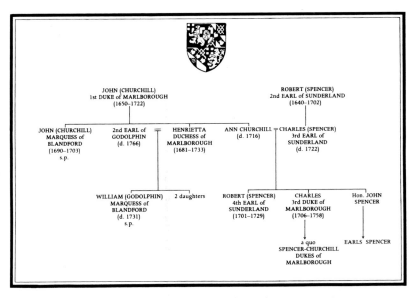

The extract from a family tree shows how the surname Spencer-Churchill arose. Charles Spencer, 3rd Earl of Sunderland married the younger daughter of John Churchill, 1st Duke of Marlborough. Following the death of her elder sister without surviving male heirs, the dukedom together with the names Spencer and Churchill came to the second son of the Earl of Sunderland. The earl's youngest son continues to use the name Spencer only and was the father of the 1st Earl Spencer.

The arms shown are those of Spencer and Churchill quartered together.

City or ~~Borough~~ of _____

Parish ~~or Township~~ of *East Peckham*

PLACE	HOUSES		NAMES of each Person who abode therein the preceding Night.	AGE and SEX		PROFESSION, TRADE, EMPLOYMENT, or of INDEPENDENT MEANS.	Where Born	
	Uninhabited or Building	Inhabited		Males	Females		Whether Born in same County	Whether Born in Scotland, Ireland, or Foreign Parts
			Ann Grayland		15	F S ✗	yes	
Kexie House		1	Thomas Martin	35		Farmer	yes	
			Maria do		30		do	
			Edwin do	5			do	
			Emily do		2		do	
			Frederick do	1 month			do	
			Ann Batchler		20	F S ✗	do	
			Caroline Colegate		20	F S ✗	do	
			Louisa Ecall		20	F S ✗	do	
			William Greenaway	25		M S ✗	do	
			Henry Jupp	18		M S ✗	do	
Mount Pleasant		1	Martha Andrews		60	Independent	yes	
			William Dunk	62		M S ✗	do	
			Caroline Wilson		25	F S ✗	do	
Near the Court lodge		1	Bathaney Freeman		19	F ✗	do	
			George Scott	29		Ag Lab	yes	
			Mary do		21		do	
			Mary do		3		do	
			Elizabeth do		2		do	
			Harriott do		2 month		do	
			Sarah Underdown		11		do	
do		1	George Bishop	28		Ag Lab	yes	
			Harriott do		30		do	
			Robert do	8			do	
			John do	5			do	
TOTAL in Page 8	**4**			**10**	**15**			

B c

34 15

	Name of Street, Place, or Road, and Name or No. of House	Name and Surname of each Person who abode in the house, on the Night of the 30th March, 1851	Relation to Head of Family	Condition	Age of Males	Age of Females	Rank, Profession, or Occupation	Where Born	Whether Blind, or Deaf-and-Dumb
		Richard West	Servant	Un	21		Farmer Servant	Kent East Peckham	
68	Hextle House Cottage	William Japp	Head	Mar	32		Gardiner	Kent East Peckham	
		Mary Japp	Wife	Mar		42		Kent Penshurst	
		Matilda Japp	Daur	Un		9	Scholar	Kent East Peckham	
69	Pond House	Robert Lipscomb	Head	Mar	56		Farmer of 130 acres employing 6 Labourers	Kent Tunbridge	
		Elizabeth Lipscomb	Wife	Mar		56	Farmer Wife	Kent Speldhurst	
		Martha Lipscomb	Daur	Un		19	Farmer Daughter	Kent Penshurst	
		Anne Laxley	Visitor	Un		20		Kent Penshurst	
70	Hextle House	Maria Martin	Head	Wid		42	Landed Proprietor	Sussex Hove	
		Anna Martin	Daur	Un		7		Kent East Peckham	
		Leslie Martin	Son		2			Kent East Peckham	
		Caroline Sansbury	Sister			43		Sussex Hove	
		Helen Murdoch	Servant	Un		19	Governess	Middlesex St Pancras	
		Ann Saunders	Servant	Un		20	House Servant	Kent East Peckham	
		Ann Dann	do	Un		27	House Servant	Sussex Lamberhurst	
		Mary Rogers	do	Un		25	House Servant	Kent East Peckham	
		George Besant	do	Un	22		Ag Lab	Kent Wrotham	
	The End of that part of the Parish of East Peckham not included in the Trinity District Wateringbury Thomas Webb								

Total of Houses 13	Total of Persons 5 12

LEFT AND RIGHT

Comparison of these extracts from the census returns of 1841 (left) and 1851 (above) for Hextle House, East Peckham, shows that Thomas Martin died between the two dates and that his wife Maria only gave her approximate age in the earlier census, as required by the rules. In 1851 return the precise place of birth is given and the children Edwin and Emily appear to have died. Leslie's birth, which took place during 1848 or 1849, gives an indication of the approximate date of Thomas's death.

Abigal	wife of John Landemore was buried June 4
Elizabeth	wife of Robert Plummer was buried July 30
Richard	Stevens an Infant was buried August 13
Tabitha	Major Infant buried Aug 30
John	Bradly was buried Sept 14
Elizab	wife of George Baker bur: Sept 16
Elizab	wife of William Alderton was buried Sept 21
Ruth	Carvel buried October 3
William	Brundwood buried Octo 9
Ruth	Cobbin buried October 13
Ann	Bradley buried October 13
Elizab	wife of Abraham Landoll was buried October 15
Mary	Goldsmith an Infant was buried November 1
Wm	Doe Infant buried Nov 28
Robt	Arther buried Jan: 23
George	Dale buried Feb 9th

William Pawlett Curate
Abra: Wetherell
Robt Butler } Church

Anno Dni 1722

Elizab	Swan Wid: buried April 7
John	Bumpstead an Infant was buried April 21
John	Newman an Infant was buried May 1st
John	Merrial was buried July 16
John	Nichols was buried July 19
William	Brunt an Infant was buried July 26
Maynard	Doe a base begotten Child was buried August 18
John	Robinson buried Jan: 26

Abraha	Landoll buried October 4
Dinah	Bennett an Infant bur Octo 28
Francis	Goldsmith buried October 29
Elizab	Landoll an Infant buried Nov 8
John	Waller Gibson Infant buried february 14
Stephen	Row Infant buried Feb 17
Alice	Hammond an Infant was buried february 21

Chr: Grove Curate
Abraham Wetherell
Robert Butler } Church

1723

Sarah	Goldsmith buried May 28
Mary	Randoll was buried June 26
Sarah	Smith was buried July 19
Bridget	Doxter of Stanton was buried August 17
Ann	Parker Infant bur Augt 23
Charles	Medcalfe buried Sept 20
Susan	Landemore buried Sept 22
Barbara	the wife of Samuel Alderton was buried October 5
Margt	Froland buried November 4
John	Gaught an Infant buried Nov 18
John	Clarke buried November 22
Rath	Bennett an Infant was buried January 12
Ann	Newman buried Jan: 30
Wm	Crick an Infant was buried march 6
Wm	Chambers was buried march
Elizab	Crick an Infant buried march 17
Ruth	Bennett an Infant was buried march 25

Chr: Grove Curate
Abra: Wetherell
Robt Butler } Church

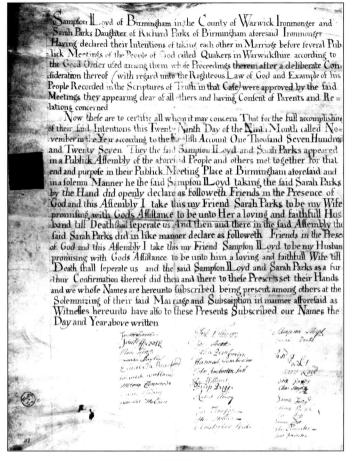

ABOVE

This Quaker marriage certificate of 1727 gives more information than is found on the Church of England marriage entries of the same date. Note that the names of the witnesses, many of whom could be related to the bride or groom, are given.

LEFT

A typical eighteenth-century country parish register from Ickworth, Suffolk showing burials for part of the period 1721-1723. Later in the century special printed registers were produced in which particulars were recorded uniformly throughout England and Wales.

and my bodie to bee buried in the parish Church yarde of Wadsworth and for my worldly goods
& estate as followeth Item I giue vnto Laurence Crump my yongest sonne fiue poundes Item
I giue vnto William Dinnis my first widowe sonne one Ewe and her lambe Item I giue vnto
James Crump my sonne two poundes and one Ewe and his lambe Item I giue vnto
Mary James Daughter to William Dinnis Com shillings Item I giue to the grosse poore
widowes & others in the Collection euery one of them one peck of wheate and Rye
the rest of my goods not disposed of my debts being paid my funerall Expences discharged
I make and ordayne Alice my wife sauande and Laurence my sonne full Executors of
this my last will and testament these being witnesses Peter Burnham Wilford Cooke
James Crump his marke

The second

day of Nouember in the yeare of our Lord God one thousand
sixe hundred fifty vnder these issued forth Letters of Administracion vnto Laurence
Crump the grandfather of James and Laurence Crump minors the somme and
surviving Executors named in the will of the sayd deceased according to the tenor and
effect of the sayd will during the minoritie and to the use of the sayd Minors then being
by vertue of a Commission in that behalfe issued forth first sworne truely to Administer
the same

In the name of God Amen

the first day of
Maye in the yeare of our Lord God according to the Computacion of the Church of England
one thousand sixe hundreth fifty and two of Henry Carver of Wadsworth in Deane
in the County of Yorke yeoman being of sounde and perfect memory and vnder=
standing and considering and well waying the frayltie and instability of this present
life doe make and ordeyne this my last will and testament in manner and forme following
That is to say first and principally I Commit my soule into the handes of Almighty God
my maker assuredly trusting in and through the meritts of our Lord and sauiour Iesus
Christ to bee one of that blessed Company to whome the Lord in full sentence (Come ye
blessed of my father Receiue the kingdome prepared for ye) shall bee pronounced And
my bodie I Committ to Christian buriall at the discretion of my kindred & freindes and
thereon And as touching the disposition of my temporall Estate which God of his goodnes
hath lent vnto mee and for the avoiding of all difference that might after my decease aruse
about the same my will and mynde is as followeth first whereas I haue already giuen and
bestowed vpon Henry Carver and John Carver my two yonger sonnes the summe of fowre
hundreth poundes a peece in liew & compens one and full satisfaction of their childs parts and
portions according as appeares by a generall release under their handes bearing date the first day of
October one thousand sixe hundred fortie and eight 1648 Co wytsome also I haue giuen
either of them one hundred poundes of Currant English money to better and Increase their
sayd childs parts and portions And whereas I haue also giuen and delivered vnto Mary Carver
my daughter in liew of her childs part and portion for which sayd debt the sayd Hugh Carver
hath sealed and Entred two severall bonds or writings obligatorie for the payment thereof
accordingly And whereas I haue already giuen and bestowed vpon Anne Watson my daughter the summe of two hundred and fifty poundes in liew compens and full satisfaction of her childs part and portion as by a generall release dated the last day of Ianuary
in the yeare of our Lord God one thousand sixe hundred forty and nyne sealed and delivered
vnto mee by William Watson her husband more fully appeareth And whereas I haue likewise giuen and bestowed vpon Martha Bardin my daughter the summe
of fiue hundred poundes sterling in liew compens and full satisfaction of her childs part
and portion as by a generall release sealed and delivered vnto mee by Edmund Bardin
her husband bearing date the eight day of July in the yeare of our Lord God one thousand
sixe hundred and fifty more fully may appeare Nowe therefore my will and mynde is
that all such debts as shall ouer at my death bee paid and disposed out of my whole
personall Estate And after payment thereof my will and mynde is And I doe hereby giue
and bequeath vnto the aforenamed Mary Carver my daughter the summe of three
hundred

Est: Henuiti Carver

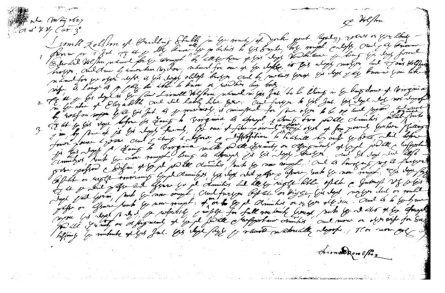

ABOVE

The deposition of a witness in a case brought before the Chancery
Court on 4 May 1627. Lionel Rolston describes how he was living
in Virginia and how, before he went, he received certain annuities
from his friends. He gives his age as 37. (Class C.24).

OPPOSITE

The Will of Henry Currer of Kildwick, Yorkshire, 1652. This is part
of the register copy in the Prerogative Court of Canterbury.

their relationship to the deceased are given. These registers also show the name of the deceased, the date of the will, the place and date of probate, the name, address and occupation of the executors, details of the estates, legacies, annuities and the duty paid.

To find out whether an estate was the subject of litigation, references should be made to the Register Books (Calendars) PROB 12. In *some* of these volumes *some* of the causes are indicated by an entry 'By Sent' (By Sentence) or 'By Decree' as a marginal note by the name of the deceased. Only in the Acts of Court Books (PROB 19) and the loose Acts (PROB 33) is there a mention of every case which came before the court. From 1660 to 1782 (PROB 3, 4, 5, 13 and 16), 1782 to 1852 (PROB 31) and before 1660 (PROB 2) records of inventories can be found. These PROB numbers should be checked as they are subject to amendment and additions.

The Irish Public Record Office in Dublin has consolidated indexes of wills and administrations from all Irish courts from October 1829 to 1879 and abstracts from 1829 to 1839, originating in the Inland Revenue Office.

12

LAND AND TAX RECORDS

◆

Although the number of people who own their own house is greater today than it has ever been, the fact remains that the records attached to land ownership and tenancies generally provide a valuable source of genealogical information.

Records of this cover a large range of sources spanning a thousand years or more of history. Probably the best known of all is the Domesday Book, a survey of his kingdom ordered by William the Conqueror in 1086. The Norman system of land tenure was based upon military service, and to ensure an effective army land was granted in return for knight-service defined in terms of quotas of armed men. The inventory of his kingdom was made so that the King could know not only the number of towns, villages and manors he and his barons possessed, but also their revenue and population. It was carried through with a degree of thoroughness unequalled until modern times, and the feudal system it established endured for several centuries. However, within each estate (called a 'manor') tenancies continued in a way which had begun before the Normans arrived.

Essentially there were two types of manorial tenant, those who were free and those who were villeins or 'bondmen'. In his turn the Lord of the Manor held his land from a higher noble who held his land from the King in return for military service. Free tenants gave military service or paid rent, villeins had the use of the land in return for work on the lord's land. In time both the Crown and the lords of the manor found it more convenient to commute both the military and farming services for money and to hire men to do the work required to run their estates or to fight their battles. The villeins' land was held according to the custom of the manor, and its transfer from one tenant to another, frequently on the death of a tenant when it would usually pass to his son, was recorded in the Court Rolls of the manor. The tenant's evidence of title was by a copy of this, thus the term 'copyhold' tenure. But the Manor Court did not confine itself to matters to do with the transfers of tenancies only. Such officers as the reeves, tithingmen and haywards were appointed annually by the Manor Courts, which also dealt with the enforcement of the customs of the manor, the punishment of petty misdemeanours, and the settlement of minor disputes between tenants and neighbours. It is obvious, therefore, that if you can identify the manor your ancestors were living on, and if the manorial records have survived, you could discover a wealth of valuable information.

To find out whether manorial sources have survived for the particular manor in which you are interested, you can consult the Manorial Documents Register at Quality House, London, which is maintained by the Royal Commission on Historical Manuscripts on behalf of the Master of the Rolls. The sections on Wales and Yorkshire are computerized and can be consulted online; for other areas you can either consult the index in London or send a written request for information, provided the enquiry concerns only one or two manors or a single parish. Local record offices will of course have a catalogue to any surviving manorial documents they hold, but as some landowners owned hundreds of manors in different parts of the country, the records may not be held locally.

Coming nearer to our own day, title deeds, Land Tax Assessments, mortgages, Hearth Tax returns, Window Tax returns, Enclosure Awards, tontines and annuities, insurance and tithe records all yield a vast amount of information about all manner of people in all walks of life, and not only the so-called landed gentry.

Similarly connections between families and between different generations of a single family can be deduced from a study of title deeds enrolled on the Close Rolls (Public Record Office), which extend back to the twelfth century. These generally concern grants of land and privileges by the Crown to individuals and corporations including monasteries, chantries and charities. In 1599, for example, Peter Page bought land from William Kirkeby of East Hatfield, Yorkshire, yeoman, which had formerly been part of the lands of the Yorkshire Priory of Nunkeeling. Deeds in the Close Rolls showed that this land had formerly belonged to Roger Kirkeby and that it had descended to his son Christopher who had died without issue, and that then it came to William, Christopher's younger brother, then to William's son Roger in 1582.

In the Close Rolls for 1630 a deed is recorded between Martin Button of Bath and Capt. Robert Kirby of Woodbridge in Suffolk on one part and Sir William Withipoll and his son, Francis, on the other. Among the lands included in this transaction, which mainly concerned the estate of Sir William Read of Osterley Park, in Middlesex, were some which formed part of the lands of Nunkeeling Priory.

The common factor between these two transactions was of course Nunkeeling Priory, for there was otherwise nothing to connect Capt. Robert Kirby of Suffolk with William Kirkeby of Yorkshire. However, on closer investigation it was discovered that the Nunkeeling Priory estate was bought at the dissolution of the monasteries by Sir Richard Gresham and John Thynne of Bath. Sir Richard Gresham's great-niece was Lady Rebecca Seckford, whose granddaughter was the wife of Robert Kirby of Woodbridge. Robert Kirby's great-grandfather, Andrew Kirby, according to heraldic evidence, came from a family settled since the tenth century in Lancashire, whose branches extended into Yorkshire.

Land records, therefore, can be invaluable in providing information about families from which much additional information can be deduced. They can also tell us much about the day-to-day lives of our ancestors, and especially about fluctuations in their fortunes. Most of these records were written in Latin up to 1732, which can be a problem for the amateur researcher.

While it is possible to use title deeds as genealogical sources without knowing much or anything about the law of real property, it is, all the same, advisable to have a passing acquaintance with the law. It must be realized, for example, that fines and recoveries represent fictitious transactions aimed at circumventing certain statutory prohibitions on the transfer of title. Similarly, a conveyance by lease and release was devised for a specific purpose. N. W. Alcock's *Old Title Deeds* provides a useful overview of the subject.

Basically, a conveyance of land is between two parties, a party in this context being one or more individuals. A deed may be a simple conveyance of a freehold interest in land from A to B or a lease for a term of years from C to D, or be increasingly complex in conveying extensive estates, creating trusts, remainders and entails for generations to come. The more complex the conveyance the greater the chances of finding genealogical information, for earlier deeds and transactions will be recited and set out, and relationships may be traceable backward for several generations. A series of deeds, both simple and complex, dealing with the same property over a number of years can give a very great deal of information about a family if the property remained in its hands throughout the period. Since it was not uncommon in Britain for families to own property for two or more centuries, the accumulation of deeds and conveyances over this period, even for quite minor families, can be extremely large.

The series of documents known as Feet of Fines (Public Record Office) not only cover an unbroken period of more than six centuries, but have no parallel in the records of any other country except perhaps some archives in Edinburgh. Beginning at the end of the twelfth century, they continue into the nineteenth. These were records of fictional law-suits over possession of land to obtain the judgement of the court as to ownership, which was a 'watertight' title. Fines were written in triplicate on parchment. The 'foot', which is the official copy of the document, was retained in the court records and still survives. A typical example, in translation, might read as follows:

This is the final agreement made in the Court of our Lord the King at Westminster in the quindene of Easter in the 7th year of the reign of King Henry VII before A.B, C.D, E.F, Justices of our Lord the King and others there present, etc. between W.X the demandant and Y.Z the deforciant of 8 acres of land and 2 acres of meadow with their appurtenances in Waxham concerning which an assize of mort d'auncestor was summoned between them in the aforesaid Court. Namely that the said Y.Z granted to the said W.X and his heirs all the aforesaid land. To hold to him and his heirs paying therefore yearly 6*d*. for all service.

And the said W.X for this grant gives the said Y.Z three shillings.

Similar records useful in medieval genealogy are the Curia Regis Rolls, De Banco Rolls, and Docket Books of the Exchequer. Another extremely valuable type of enquiry was that which was conducted after the death of many landowners, known as an Inquisition Post Mortem (IPM). On the death of such a man, an enquiry was held to determine the extent and location of his land, and the terms under which he held it. This usually elicits the date of the tenant's death and the name, age and relationship of the next heir. Unfortunately these enquiries ceased in 1645 and were not renewed at the Restoration.

During the English Civil War, landowners who supported the King against the victorious Commonwealth had their lands confiscated by order of committees appointed to investigate the actions of the owners. Having 'confessed their delinquency' and given a pledge to adhere to the Commonwealth, they had to give a full account of their possessions and were then allowed to 'compound' by surrendering a portion of their estate, which varied according to their 'guilt'. The records of these committees (PRO Class SP/23) give a lot of information about the condition of such individuals, often mentioning their heirs and other members of their family. They are known as Composition Papers.

Exchequer Class E 179, at the Public Record Office, are records of tax assessments. Among these, the 'Lay Subsidies' are useful because they give the names of taxpayers at the level of wealth taxed that year. They are listed by years and 'hundred' divisions of counties. Also in this class of document are the Hearth Tax returns of Charles II's reign, many of which have been published by local historical societies, and other lists of taxpayers such as some Poll Tax returns. The lists include not only those who paid the tax, but also those who were exempted from paying on account of poverty. This is the only comprehensive list of householders in the late seventeenth century. Unfortunately not all assessments have survived, but these returns are a primary source well worth consulting. In addition to telling you whether an ancestor of yours was in the parish at the time of the tax return, the published returns indicate in which areas of the county a surname was found, which can be very useful when you have lost track of a family.

A particularly useful adjunct to subsidy records is in the class E 115 at the Public Record Office; these are certificates of residence for subsidy, and their main value is in effect as a record of 'change of address' where a taxpayer moves away.

13

RECORDS OF THE SERVICES AND PROFESSIONS

Most service records are kept at the Public Record Office, Kew, and many of the printed sources are available at local reference libraries.

NAVAL RECORDS

Seamen's lives are often depicted as adventurous, daring and exciting. However, underneath the glamour there was another side. There were people who chose the Navy as their career voluntarily, but there were many more who were literally pressed into the 'King's Navy' for what would seem to us a pittance. Conditions were harsh. This was particularly true for those who were below deck. For those above, life was not absolutely cosy either.

The abundance of records that exist shed a great deal of light on these men's lives. Some records give such personal details as what they looked like and even what they ate! This chapter gives a brief summary of those records of particular genealogical interest which are available.

For men serving before the Restoration (1660) no systematic records survive but mentions of individuals on ships are to be found in printed *Calendars of State Papers, Domestic* (Public Record Office).

Commissioned Officers

Histories of sea officers' careers can be found in printed books as well as manuscript sources. Taking printed sources one must mention Steele's *Navy List* (from 1782 onwards) followed by the Navy List (quarterly from 1814 onwards), Charnock's *Biographia Navalis* (1794–8), Marshall's *Royal Naval Biography* (1823–30) and O'Byrne's *A Naval Biographical Dictionary* (1849) describing all officers serving in the Navy in 1834. There is also the *Commissioned Sea Officers of the Royal Navy (1660–1815)* published by the National Maritime Museum which presents the dates when officers joined certain ranks. The first manuscript record to look for is the Lieutenant's passing certificate which, depending where you find it, gives you a copy of his baptismal certificate and summarizes his previous training and career.

If you are unlucky enough not to find your man here try and find his Record of Service which will give the dates when he served on a particular ship. From this you can look up the ships' Muster Rolls when he was serving as a Midshipman or as an Able Seaman to seek his place of birth.

Warrant Officers

This term means that they were seamen but were under receipt of warrants. Up to some point in the nineteenth century the commissioned officers were not men who actually navigated ships; this was left to those who were known as the Masters and their Mates. Formally they were only classed as Warrant Officers together with pursers, gunners, engineers, carpenters and boatswains, more commonly known as bosuns. There should be some record for all of these although not all have survived.

Ratings

Before the mid-nineteenth century, generally speaking, it is necessary to know in what ship a man was serving at a particular time. You then use the Muster Rolls which will give details as previously described as well as the ship in which he last served and the date he was discharged from that ship.

From 1853 'Continuous Service Engagement' was introduced. Seamen were given numbers and thus a record of services followed which gives the date and place of birth as well as a physical description and a list of the ships in which he served. For the really ardent researcher there is no end to the length to which he can pursue his studies, like looking up the ships' logs and learning of every single event that occurred in this particular ship. Some of the details may be repetitive like the exact geographical situation of the ship at a particular time of day and the climate, but these logs also record such happenings as 'Seaman Bloggs was insubordinate to an officer, received a hundred lashes on the deck and was sent below.'

These records of services continue up to 1891 and are compiled from when seamen actually joined the navy. For any records of service of seamen who joined after that date, direct descendants can write to the Naval and Army Records Centre.

Naval Records for Genealogists by N. A. M. Rodger (Public Record Office 1988) is a useful additional guide. Information about naval personnel who served after 1891 can be obtained from the Naval Personnel Records, Room 2007, OS9(a), Ministry of Defence, Empress State Buildings, London SW6 1TR, and in some cases from the National Maritime Museum, Greenwich SE10 9NF.

The Marines

By an Order-in-Council in 1664 what are now known as the Royal Marines was founded. They were men who not only sailed in ships but also fought on land and therefore were responsible to both the Navy and the Army. Officers' records are in the Admiralty Series. For other ranks you can find your man according to which division he was stationed in; these were at Chatham, Woolwich, Portsmouth and Plymouth. You begin by searching the Description Books and from these you can go on to look for a record of service.

After 1901 records concerning men and officers who served in the Marines are kept in the Royal Marine Drafting and Record Office, HMS Centurion, Grange Road, Portsmouth PO13 9XA.

Debrett's Guide to Tracing Your Family Tree

Coastguards

Coastguards were men drafted from the Navy beginning about 1816. Here all you need know to begin your research is which station a man was serving at a particular time. From there you can trace all kinds of records from his last ship in the Royal Navy to his date of discharge. Coastguards were administered by the Navy but paid for by the Customs. Therefore, a word of warning: sometimes a man will be described on marriage certificates as a Customs officer when he in fact was a Coastguard.

MILITARY RECORDS

Before the Civil Wars (1642–9) there was no regular standing army in England. Regiments were raised to meet a particular requirement and were known by the name of the colonels who formed them. No systematic records of such regiments survive though references to individual officers and soldiers can be found in State Papers Domestic, Foreign, and other records at the Public Record Office and the Manuscript Department of the British Library.

After the Restoration (1660) records became more abundant, but do not really contain much biographical information of officers and men which is of use to the researcher until the nineteenth century.

A useful guide for those interested in military records is a Public Record Office publication entitled *Army Records for Family Historians* (1998). Other useful publications are Gerald Hamilton-Edwards, *In Search of Army Ancestry* (1977), and N. Holding, *World War One Army Ancestry* (1982) and its supplement (1991).

Many First World War army records were destroyed by bombing during the Second World War. Records that have survived are gradually being released; some are pensions records, relating to those who were injured or killed, and some are service records. More recent Army records will only be released to next-of-kin and application should be made to the Ministry of Defence, CS(R)2b, Bourne Avenue, Hayes, Middlesex UB3 1RS. For those who served in the Royal Artillery, information can be got from the RA Record and Manning Office, Imphal Barracks, York YO1 4HD. Additional information can be obtained from the National Army Museum, Royal Hospital Road, London SW3 4HT, and from the Army

Museums Ogilby Trust, Ministry of Defence (Army), 85 Whitehall, London SW1A 2NP. In addition, most regiments have their own museums, some of which contain useful archives.

Officers

Service records of commissioned officers of the British Army can be traced with only approximate completeness from the year 1660. From the mid-eighteenth century preliminary details can be obtained from Army Lists but family details can be found to be only satisfactory if the officer was serving after 1829. There are the Commander-in-Chief's memorandum papers which begin in 1793. Frankly this is over-emphasized as a useful source. Sometimes you can find a letter of recommendation containing family background but experience shows this is the exception rather than the rule. There are returns of officers' service 1808–10, but these give no personal details and only include the ranks of General down to Major.

In 1829 systematic records of services were introduced which were arranged by regiments and these unfortunate officers, of which there were many, were placed on half pay. Both they and their counterparts in the Royal Navy suffered because of the vast reduction of the armed services after the Napoleonic Wars. These records contain place of birth, details of service career, details of marriage, spouse and children, if any, with their dates of birth. You should be able to find such records up to about 1870. Thereafter one has to rely on Army Lists.

Other Ranks

Here you can be more hopeful. The first source one recommends are the soldier discharge papers which cover the years from 1756 to 1913. These are useful only if your man was discharged on a pension, not if he died on active service or if he deserted. Equally it is necessary to know the name of the regiment in which he served until 1873. From then until 1883 the papers are arranged separately for the cavalry, infantry, artillery, and so on. It is only from then onwards you find all discharge certificates, except for those who died, in one long alphabetical series for the whole Army.

These papers contain much information: the place of birth, the age of the soldier when he enlisted, his physical description, previous occupation and intended place of residence on discharge. They also give details of his career and conduct. Furthermore, some show medical details which can be very illuminating especially if he was somewhat intemperate or committed an indiscretion and suffered accordingly. Some of the later papers go even further by giving traces of next of kin, of marriage and of children.

Other series which give you vital information are the Regimental Description Books, whose survival is somewhat precarious, and the Casualty Returns. If all else fails you can search the Muster Rolls and trace a man's activities month by month. Sometimes here you can find personal details. For example, a search was made to find one James Ashley in a certain infantry regiment. There was no Record of Service for him and the Description Book was missing. After a fifteen-year search in the Muster Rolls it was discovered that he and his wife died in a yellow fever epidemic in Bermuda. This disaster occurred as the disease spread from a prison hulk moored off the island where it began and thereupon it raged all around. His two orphans were sent back to England and put into the Duke of York's Military School. They stayed there for just over a year before they were sent to a maternal uncle in Australia. The reader will be left in no doubt that to find this information was a triumph.

Militia

This ancient body is best described as a part-time army raised when needed. Today it is best known as the Territorial Army. The first series of Muster Rolls dates from 1522–1640. Some of these records are to be found in the Public Record Office, others in private muniments, others still in county record offices. You are likely to get information on names only, but even that is helpful in this period. A number of these Muster Rolls have been published by local record societies.

The Militia was very active during the Napoleonic Wars when a large part of the regular army was abroad. Most recent records that have survived are in the form of Muster Rolls as described above, but there are some other records.

Royal Flying Corps and Royal Air Force

Although the RFC was part of the Army before and during the First World War, RAF records date from the service's foundation at the end of that war. Some early records are at the Public Record Office in the Paymaster General's Records and among those of the Air Ministry and Foreign Office. In the main, however, they can be obtained from RAF Personnel Management Centre, RAF Innsworth, Gloucester GL3 1EZ. RFC records are at the Ministry of Defence at Hayes, Middlesex, with possible extra information from the Imperial War Museum, Duxford, Cambridgeshire, and the Air Force Museum at Hendon.

MERCANTILE MARINE

The whole of the merchant service was controlled by the Department of the Board of Trade, and under this body was the Registrar General of Shipping and Seamen whose records we are concerned with. Those of genealogical interest begin for seamen who served after 1835. Although from 1747 Masters or owners of ships were obliged to keep Muster Rolls of each voyage made, in which were entered the names of officers and seamen, only a few of these survive up to 1835 when a new system known as 'The Agreements and Crew Lists' was introduced. In the first series, 1835–44, you can find details of age and place of birth only. The next series, 1845–53, when the system of seamen's tickets was introduced, is the only one of real value. Here you find place and date of birth, with physical descriptions and the nicety as to whether the seaman could read or write together with his shore residence.

The ticketing system proved unpopular with seamen and the administration involved outweighed the information gained, so it was abolished in October 1853. Thus a new register was introduced, but in 1856 the department was satisfied that the Crew Lists sufficed and so that, too, was abolished. Thereafter, unless you know a man's ship together with its port of origin, you will have a difficult task in tracing him.

For Master Mariners and Mates, Certificates of Competency were issued as a result of the Merchant Ship Act of 1850. These registers contain the place and date of birth and the port where the certificate was issued. You should find your man here if he was certificated before 1900.

All the above records are at the Public Record Office, Kew. From 1857 the system changed, so check what is available at Kew and what may be at the National Maritime Museum, Greenwich. For further information about ordinary seamen after 1870 and officers after 1913 you should contact the Registrar General of Shipping and Seamen, Llantrisant Road, Llandaff, Cardiff CF5 2YS.

CUSTOMS AND EXCISE

The Boards of Customs and Excise were not amalgamated until 1910. The Customs were responsible for controlling the revenue at ports and the Excise men were responsible for seeing duties were paid.

Some personal details of Customs officers can be found, but records for many at the ports of London and Liverpool have been destroyed.

For Excise men there is a magnificent collection of Board Minute Books dating from 1688 that continue up to the late nineteenth century. From these we can trace a man's career from when he started as a supernumerary until his discharge or death. Often we find that a man followed in his father's footsteps and his own sons followed suit. There are also some entry papers which give personal details of men who joined the services after 1820.

RAILWAYMEN

A railway enthusiast can have a beanfeast at the Public Record Office where he can find a multitude of original records together with many printed histories and periodicals. This mass of stuff deals with every aspect of railway organization which varied from company to company, particularly when it comes to staff records. Regarding the staff records, their usefulness varies and to search them can be frustrating. One only has to use them when you lose a railwayman in records like the Census Returns. Railwaymen obviously were moved about. Often if you are looking for an engine driver in one company you find only the station staff records have survived or vice versa. However, do not be daunted by this and have a go at them if you feel fit to do so. With these records you will also find some for the Inland Waterways. Bargemen and their families are usually elusive to say the least.

THE GENERAL POST OFFICE

Anyone who is looking for a postmaster or letter carrier, which a postman was formerly known as, can go to the General Post Office record room in London to see what he can find. There are registers of correspondence to look at as well as other material which is interesting, if not biographical. Often you can find reference to a particular person in one form or another. However, searching in this area is not particularly productive.

All the service records listed above, apart from those to do with the postal services who retain their own records, are housed in the Public Record Office at Kew.

PROFESSIONS AND TRADES

If your ancestor did belong to one of the professions or trades, it does not necessarily mean that you are going to have an easy path in tracing him, though it is worth taking up the challenge. Before describing the cross-section, it is recommended that you make one or two reference checks in printed sources. The first of these is to consult the University Alumni. Most ancient universities have published details of their former students back to the sixteenth century. In England there are two publications, namely the Oxford and Cambridge Alumni (J. Foster, *Alumni Oxoniensis 1500–1886* and J. A. Venn, *Alumni Cantabrigiensis*). The details you will find in these records are the names of the father, his rank and occupation, where the student lived, his college and his later career if known.

If you fail here you can try the Dublin Alumni, and following this the printed books of the four old Scottish universities. Sometimes one can be very lucky in one's searches of these records and find whole generations of families.

Many public schools, too, have published records which can be consulted.

Clergy

Practically all clergy of the Church of England in former years went to either Oxford or Cambridge. The famous *Crockford's* was first published in 1848. Before this date there were Clergy Lists as well as ordination papers which are kept in the diocesan office of the See in which the priest was ordained.

You will find records of the Nonconformist clergymen among the records of their particular denominations. However, the best place to start is to look at a card index in the Dr Williams Library in London which gives you details of mainly Independent and Congregational clergymen. These usually give some details of their background and you can sometimes find their photograph and references to their funeral sermons as well. Similarly for a Baptist minister you go to the Baptist Union where again they have their own card index. For Methodists and others there are details at The John Rylands University Library, Deansgate, Manchester M3 3EH. University Alumni records (see above) are also useful for clergy families.

Medical Profession

Early material concerning doctors is really rather sketchy. There are a few records at the libraries of the Royal Colleges of Physicians and Surgeons. Curiously enough few doctors went to English universities. They were trained either in Edinburgh or at Leyden in Holland.

The first medical directory was published in 1847 and in 1849 a system of medical registration was set up with the *Medical Register* being published annually from 1858 onwards. The entries show their qualifications and the place where they were practising. They may have been members of the Barber Surgeons' Company or members of the Society of Apothecaries. In 1815 licenciates of the latter society were introduced which covered apothecaries all over the country. Today we think of apothecaries as pharmacists or chemists but at that time practically all doctors would have had that qualification. Looking at the records you will see that the courses they attended covered a much wider area than basic chemistry.

Biographies of the Fellows of the Royal College of Physicians were published from 1518 as *Munk's Roll of Physicians*. Fellows of the Royal College of Surgeons (founded 1800) are described in *Lives of the Fellows of the Royal College of Surgeons*. The records of the Society of Apothecaries, founded in 1617, are at the Guildhall Library, London.

Legal Professions

Barristers when called to the Bar became members of one of the four Inns of Court. They all have published records of their members. If you want further information you can always apply to the library of the particular Inn. Solicitors and barristers are recorded in the annual *Law Lists*, published since 1775. To find more detailed information there are also indentures at the Public Record Office for men who were attached to the Court of Common Pleas and the King's Bench.

Apprenticeship

Apprenticeship for trades and professions dates back in some cases to the Middle Ages. Livery Companies and Guilds were formed particularly in the City of London and in some of the major trading cities such as Bristol, Exeter, York and Newcastle. They laid down standards of workmanship for their craft. As a result young men were bound to masters of the trade concerned for periods varying from five to nine years after which they became freemen of the company.

Many of these records have survived and for London many have been deposited at the Guildhall Library, while others are still in the Halls of the companies concerned, e.g. the Goldsmiths' and Stationers' companies, where you can apply direct for information. Similar records exist for the provincial guilds.

The apprentice-binding registers usually give the name, address and trade of the apprentice and address of the master. Besides being apprenticed it was possible to become a freeman of a company by redemption which meant that you paid a fee, having satisfied the Livery of your capabilities.

If you are not sure to which company your ancestor belonged, you are encouraged to go in person to the city chamberlain's office to search the freedoms admission register, or failing this, apply in writing.

It is important to note that from the beginning of the nineteenth century a man could belong to a company different from that of his trade, i.e. a fishmonger could belong to the Drapers' Company.

Besides these sources there is an index of details of apprentices compiled by Perceval Boyd from Inland Revenue records, copies of which are kept at the Society of Genealogists and the Guildhall Library. This is presented in two series, namely 1710–60 and 1761–72. Between the latter date and 1809 you can wade through the registers in the Public Record Office which are unindexed. These do not include poor law apprentices which are mentioned in Chapter 7.

RECORDS OF THE BRITISH IN INDIA

There is a considerable collection of personal records of the East India Company and later of the Indian Empire at the India Record Office and Library. This contains details of the Civil Service and the Army, as well as other personnel living in the subcontinent.

For those interested in Indian Service Records of the Honourable East India Company or the Indian Army, application should be made to the Oriental and India Office Collections at the British Library, but the records of the regular Army in India are with the other Army records at the Public Record Office, Kew. See also *The British Overseas* (Guildhall Library Research Guide 3rd ed.).

14

EMIGRATION

NORTH AMERICA

For an American of European descent, the attempt to identify emigrant ancestors requires much preliminary work in America before searches can be undertaken profitably in Europe. He must discover when his ancestor's name first appears in American records; who were the emigrant's closest associates; whether he was a trapper, planter or professional man; to what religious or ethnic group he belonged; whether he remained in one city or state all his life; whether his children married within the local community or outside it; if he was a man of property – can any clue to his origin be gained from knowing the name he gave his home or plantation? to whom was he related by blood and marriage? These and other seemingly trivial questions must be answered before one can hope to identify him in Europe. Furthermore, the problem of finding these answers varies from state to state and from one century to another; thus a knowledge of how the states of America were settled is essential.

North America from the Gulf of Mexico to the Arctic has been

111

populated by migrants who arrived over a period of nearly four hundred years beginning in the late sixteenth century. Broadly speaking, those who settled on the eastern coastal plains between latitudes thirty-five degrees and fifty degrees north were English, Dutch, Scandinavian and French in origin. At first they occupied a fairly narrow belt of land bounded in the west by the Appalachians and the Great Lakes. South of thirty-five degrees, which embraces Florida and the West Indies, the settlements were mainly Spanish, interspersed with settlements of French, Dutch and English. The Mississippi valley was a French preserve, west of which ranged the vast Spanish empire of Central America, consisting not only of modern Mexico and all the states to its south-east, but also Texas and California as far north as latitude forty degrees. Not until the nineteenth century was the remainder of the landmass settled by Europeans in a movement of population which continues today.

Within this huge area of space and time, the pattern and rate of migration has been regulated by economic, political and religious factors, operating not only within Europe itself, but also within its individual countries and their provinces. Migration is hardly ever a matter of free, unfettered choice; there are always factors that drive as well as attract. To the well-to-do, America offered opportunities to the enterprising. To the less well off it promised land and work; to the poor, the petty criminal and the member of unpopular minorities, there was virtually no choice, unless it was one between death or prison at home and exile abroad. During the past two hundred years, most European migrants have gone to America under some kind of duress. By contrast, the promoters of the London Virginia Company proclaimed in 1610 the advantages of colonization and emigration as being three in number: first, to preach Christianity to the pagan natives; second, to relieve overcrowding at home; and, lastly, to obtain fruitful land on which to grow products for export to Europe.

To settle colonies you need not only leaders but labourers and the motives of those who commanded were very different from those who had to obey. So the attraction of America to the French

Huguenot or English Brownist was quite different from that which motivated the Dutch or English merchant. Genealogists, therefore, must be aware of such differences when they attempt to identify particular emigrants. Because most emigrants were from humble stations in life, and because, in England especially, there were numerous people bearing identical names, it is probable that identification will only be by means of circumstantial, rather than direct, evidence.

British settlement in North America began very simply. Various groups settled along the northern half of the east coast – now essentially in what is known as New England – and along the southern coast to the north of Florida. This area was loosely termed Virginia, a far wider area than the modern state of that name.

Contrary to general popular belief, North America was not first colonized by the passengers who sailed in the *Mayflower* in 1620. The earliest permanent colony was founded at Jamestown, in Virginia, in 1607. The main impetus to settlement came from the pressure of primogeniture (whereby the eldest son inherited the lion's share of the family property) upon younger sons of the landed, merchant and professional classes. Much of the early labour force came as indentured servants through the ports of Bristol and London, and quite a few records survive of their names and the length of time they had to serve. The southern states operated the 'headright' system, whereby anyone who paid the fare of a passenger to people the colony was entitled to a grant of fifty acres of land. Although there were cases of abuse, the system generated lists of persons arriving in the colony, a source of great value if you understand that the date of a grant supported by such a list could often mean that those whose names appear on it came several years earlier. The richer planters would purchase headrights as well as claim them for passengers they had brought themselves, and in the case of some of the larger plantations, these lists run to several hundred names collected over as long a period as ten to twelve years.

New England, on the other hand, was largely colonized by groups of religious dissidents. There was, for example, a

Cambridge-based Puritan group, drawing members from as far away as Yorkshire and Kent; groups from Dorchester, Plymouth and to a lesser extent Bristol. These were attracted as much by the fine cod-fisheries as by the chance to practise their religion freely. The origins of many of these immigrants can be traced by identifying the group to which they belonged, though it has to be emphasized that, being religious in character, they attracted members from all over the country. On the other hand, those who exported indentured servants to Virginia usually recruited them in their home districts, so it is important to establish from where in England the planter who claimed the headright came before starting to look for the places of origin of his servants.

It is obviously impossible to cover this large subject in a short chapter such as this, but groups of intermarried kin from south Yorkshire, East Anglia, Kent and London can be identified, and colonies like Maryland (Catholic) and Pennsylvania (Quaker) offer clues to where searches should be started.

With these differences in mind, it is easy to understand why the northern colonies in the seventeenth century attracted men and women from all over Britain, for their common interest was a dislike of the Established Church. This means that the genealogist must search among sectarian records rather than among the archives of a particular region, though even in New England, and particularly in Massachusetts, the majority emigrated from the south-east of England through the port of London.

The English Civil Wars of the 1640s completely changed the pattern of migration. Virginia remained loyal to the King, whereas New England supported parliament. For the first time in its history Virginia began to welcome political refugees, not only from England, but also from other transatlantic colonies. The Civil Wars ended the trading monopoly of London, and thereafter Bristol began to trade in tobacco and sugar from the Americas and to export indentured servants to the colonies. Between 1654 and 1685 the names of more than 10,000 indentured servants are to be found in the Bristol records destined for Virginia and the West Indies. During the same period, emigration to New England almost dried up completely. With this shift in the pattern of trade from London to Bristol, the recruiting ground for emigrants switched from the south-east to the Severn valley, South Wales and those regions of Wiltshire, Somerset and Dorset lying within a radius of fifty miles of Bristol.

It is a common, though erroneous, belief that once an emigrant left Europe he never returned. There is also a belief that if a name is found, say, in Barbados, it cannot possibly belong to an individual of the same name living in Virginia or New England at about the same time. While it is indeed true to say that the majority of emigrants stayed where they were once they arrived on the far side of the Atlantic, nevertheless, mobility between one colony and another, as well as back and forth across the ocean, was by no means rare, or confined to the rich, to seamen or to traders. There are numerous instances of men and women of modest means, even of servants, returning home to visit relatives or to attend to family business, in particular to matters connected with the inheritance of property.

Even though emigration in the earliest years was on the whole voluntary, nevertheless forced transportation as a punishment began as early as 1615. It has been estimated that more than 30,000 convicts were transported from England to America and the West Indies between that date and 1775. (See *The Complete Book of Emigrants in Bondage, 1614–1775* by P. W. Coldham, 1988.)

The southern and northern fringes each have different histories. The Trustees of Georgia, who founded that colony in 1732, were a group of philanthropists who sought to found a colony for debtors. Nova Scotia, on the other hand, was set up as an outpost against the French in Canada and settled largely by Scots. (For a more thorough exploration of this complicated question see T. C. C. Graham's *Colonists from Scotland, 1707–1783* 1981, E. G. Hartman's *Emigration from Wales* 1967, and N. Currer-Briggs's *Worldwide Family History* 1982.)

A good deal of work has been carried out in recent years to make the fragmented information about British emigrants to North America more accessible. Of particular importance is the ongoing *Passenger and Immigration Lists Index*, for which a supplement has been brought out annually since 1998, edited by P. William Filby and others. This provides a surname index to a vast number and variety of primary and secondary sources including passenger lists, naturalization records, colonial records and 'gleanings' from records in the home country, covering emigration from Europe to North America.

CANADA

Canada, as is generally known, was colonized by the French in the seventeenth century. Following the independence of the United States, Canada became the only British possession on the North American mainland. By 1791 six provinces had come into existence: Lower Canada, the most populous and longest settled, was over-whelmingly French; Upper Canada and New Brunswick had only just been created; the settlement of Prince Edward Island (formerly St John Island) had barely begun; Newfoundland and Nova Scotia were older British possessions. The British population of Canada differed radically from that of the thirteen colonies which had seceded. Many loyalists had fled from them to avoid persecution at the hands of American radicals, which meant that they were not only staunchly royalist but also very conservative.

Comparatively few settlers arrived in Canada before 1814, but by 1851 more than 200,000 English-speaking Americans had come to the north bank of the St Lawrence and of Lakes Ontario and Erie and to the eastern shore of Lake Huron. (For further information see *Canada – A Political and Social History* by E. McMinnis, 1985.)

AUSTRALIA AND NEW ZEALAND

European settlement here has taken place only in the last two centuries, and owes a good deal to the aftermath of the American Revolution. It was first suggested as somewhere the dispossessed Loyalists could be settled, but a greater attraction for the British Government was the fact that Australia was a place to which the convicts, who would formerly have been sent to Virginia and Maryland and who were overcrowding British prisons, could be transported.

116

So Australia began as a penal settlement when the First Fleet landed at Sydney Cove on 26 January 1788, carrying 736 convicts and 294 officers and men to govern and guard them. For the first two decades, the new arrivals were largely convicts, with a few 'gentleman settlers', often former Army officers. Transportation of convicts did not cease until 1868, but by 1820 New South Wales was no longer solely a penal settlement, and the wool trade, soon to be the mainstay of the country's economy, had begun. 200,000 free settlers arrived between 1820 and 1850 almost entirely from the British Isles, with a sprinkling of Germans. The Gold Rush began in 1851, and this led to the population trebling in thirty years. Australian emigration can be put into perspective when we learn that it was not until about 1870 that native-born Australians outnumbered immigrants, and the British and Irish element in their origins did not fall below 95 per cent until 1945. In New Zealand there was no penal settlement, and little immigration before the 1840s; the major influx came after the discovery of gold in 1861, and the proportion of British and Irish ancestry in the make-up of New Zealanders is even higher than in that of Australians.

From the family historian's point of view, the importance of this is that most of his ancestors left the British Isles in the era of modern records and they were already recorded there in civil registration of births, marriages and deaths, and in the census. In addition to this, the new colonies (as they were then) began keeping good records of their own. Not only did they introduce civil registration earlier than most European and American states, but they recorded a great deal of detail about the family, which is hard to equal anywhere else in the world as a working tool for genealogists.

Civil registration of this type began in New Zealand in 1848, and in Australia at various dates: Tasmania 1838, Western Australia and Victoria 1841, South Australia 1842, New South Wales and Queensland 1856. Before those dates, there are church registers of baptisms, marriages and burials; there are also tombstones which supply information, but these are neither as complete nor as informative as civil registration records, although Norfolk Island

117

church registers, for example, date back to 1790. As is inevitable in a developing country, and because people are only human, not every event was recorded: a death was registered by someone who got the facts wrong, or a priest performing a marriage failed to enter all of the answers on the printed form, but most Australians and New Zealanders can trace their ancestry back through registration of births, marriages and deaths to a specific place and date in the British Isles, simply from the Registrars' records, without any great difficulty. This is particularly true of those whose ancestors emigrated in the 1850s or later, although, of course, many of the earlier settlers died after civil registration had begun, and it should not be forgotten that their death certificates carry the same information.

Those who slipped through the net of the system for one reason or another, as well as earlier arrivals, present more problems. They can be classified in two groups: those who arrived as convicts and those who came as free settlers – although the two groups tend to be confused by the fact that a number of convicts' wives and families emigrated as free settlers to join their men.

In general, and perhaps ironically, the early free settlers are harder to trace than the convicts. Passenger lists of departures at the British end do not usually survive from before 1890, but Australian and New Zealand passenger arrival lists are very extensive, and *should* record families with their ages and 'native places'. They are generally classified by ship's name and by date, and many have been indexed, but for those that have not, more information is needed, as without these two facts the sheer physical task of searching the vast lists is daunting. Fortunately a lot of earlier Australian records include this information, notably censuses and Immigration Agents' lists. There was a series of censuses of New South Wales and Tasmania, some of which listed the convict population only, and others the free population as well, of which the most complete is that of 1828. British Army records can help as well, not only for the men originally sent out as garrisons and guards for the convicts, but also for those who emigrated under a government scheme to encourage Army pensioners to settle there.

Convict ancestry is no disgrace in Australia; indeed there is an exclusive club in Melbourne of which membership is limited to those with such a forebear, and an Australian takes as much pride in an ancestor on the First Fleet as does an American whose ancestor was on the *Mayflower*, but with the advantage that Australian convicts are better documented.

In terms of the technicalities of research, Australian records such as censuses, permits to marry, tickets of leave and the like usually identify convicts either by the ship they were carried in and the date of arrival, or by the date and place of conviction in Britain or Ireland. From these records, or from the Transportation Registers (which are arranged by date and indexed by ship) one can discover the Assizes or other court where the prisoner was sentenced. The reference to date and place of conviction is important, as the court records are so vast that it would be otherwise all but impossible to find the correct entry.

The court record of the crime (usually a petty one) including the evidence and conviction is usually a piece of family history in itself, even if it is not a particularly happy chapter. Often there is very little evidence in court of the birthplace of the prisoner, and naturally a great many crimes were committed away from home anyway. Of course, you can get examples like the trial of Charles Fancoat in Scotland, 1854, the record of which runs for 117 pages. Among the witnesses who appeared in testimony of his character was the clergyman from the parish 250 miles away in Staffordshire, where he had been born. More often, however, it is necessary to follow the chain of bureaucracy which comes into being after conviction and sentence, and which no legal system seems able to avoid. London is very well served with the records of the Newgate Calendar and the Old Bailey Sessions, as well as Criminal Registers starting in 1791. For the rest of the country Criminal Registers start in 1805, and list all persons charged with crimes, the outcome of the trial and the sentence. Prison records list convicts held both in prisons and in the hulks awaiting transportation; from there they can be followed through to the Transportation Registers. Usually at one or more points in the sequence of records the important facts of the age and birthplace of the convict are recorded, as well as their state of health, their behaviour and other personal details.

Most of these records are in the Public Record Office in London, although records of trials in Scotland and Ireland or English county quarter sessions are in the respective national or county record offices. Many of the major records are available on microfilm in Australia.

SOUTH AFRICA

Europeans have lived in South Africa for more than four hundred years. If the arrival of the Portuguese is taken as a starting point, European Africa has a history as long as that of Latin America; if, on the other hand, one takes the Dutch occupation of Table Bay as the beginning, South Africa has a history almost as long as that of the United States. For the purposes of this book, however, the British occupation of the lands south of the Zambezi is what concerns us. (See also E. A. Walker's *History of South Africa* 1957, and N. Currer-Briggs's *Worldwide Family History* 1982.)

The first British occupation of the Cape lasted from 1795 to 1803. At that time there were some 16,000 Europeans. This period was followed by the brief rule of the Batavian Republic (1803–6) before the second British occupation which lasted till 1823. In common with the United States, Canada, Australia and New Zealand, South Africa took its share of immigrants during the late nineteenth century and early twentieth, the reasons being the same as those which prompted migration to these other countries.

The Union of South Africa was formed in 1910, and the country left the Commonwealth in 1961. Genealogical research in South Africa is comparatively easy due to the small European population of the country before 1820, when there were only 43,000 settlers, 9,000 of whom lived in or near Cape Town. The three northern provinces of Transvaal, Natal and the Orange Free State were not opened up until the Great Trek of 1838. The first uniform law for the registration of births, deaths and marriages for the whole of South Africa was in 1923. Before 1921 each republic/colony/province had its own legislation. (See *Worldwide Family History* pp 196–206 for addresses and details of relevant legislation.)

120

The British Overseas

Mention should also be made of records of the British expatriate population, in former British colonies and elsewhere. A guide to these sources can be found in the Guildhall Library publication *The British Overseas* (3rd ed. 1995).

15

HERALDRY AND FAMILY HISTORY

◆

A basic knowledge of the principles of heraldry and of the somewhat archaic way in which arms are described is useful for those in search of their ancestry. In fact, much of heraldry can be described as pictorial genealogy, for its main purpose is to do with identification and inheritance. There is probably more non-sense and misunderstanding about heraldry than about any other aspect of genealogy and family history. Its value to the researcher is firstly to identify an individual or his immediate connections, and then to place him into the appropriate slot in a pedigree.

The origins of heraldry date from the eleventh century and arose from the need for personal identification on the battlefield and through the use of seals on legal documents. The emblems adopted for shield and seal were handed down from father to son over generations and thus became an integral part of each family's history. Shields are still used by companies and corporate bodies though almost never by individuals.

In order to introduce some order into the assumption, granting and registering of arms, colleges of heralds arose, who worked on

123

behalf of the sovereign who was generally recognized as the fount of honour. The heralds were given power to settle disputes and to legalize grants of arms and to make new grants. Every coat of arms must first have been granted, or, if it had been assumed before the institution of the College of Arms, have been recognized by or on behalf of the sovereign, and its transmission or destination (usually in the male line) follows that set out in the original patent or confirmation, just like most hereditary titles. In Scotland, only the eldest son inherits his father's arms, but all younger sons have the right to matriculate a differenced version of their paternal arms. Thus someone of the same surname as you has no more right to bear your family's arms than someone named Howard has the right to call himself Duke of Norfolk.

Most people think of heraldry as something exclusive to the nobility and gentry. In practice, however, it is not like this at all. The junior branches of some noble houses have over the space of four or five generations fallen on hard times and sunk in the social scale. Many new families have risen from humble origins and applied for grants of arms in the recent past. Social mobility, therefore, ensures that heraldry is widely disseminated.

The two main categories of importance to genealogists are familial and individual heraldry. The former is practised throughout Europe, and we shall be saying a little about continental heraldry below. Familial heraldry pertains to a family rather than to an individual, whereby all male descendants of the original grantee bear the same family arms undifferenced, in much the same way as all the children of a count of the Holy Roman Empire, for example, would be counts and countesses themselves. Such a system is only practical where there are a great many surnames, though it is a mistake to believe that there is a coat of arms for every surname.

The College of Arms in London is responsible for all aspects of English and Welsh heraldry and for much of Irish and Commonwealth heraldry too. Many Americans apply to the College for coats of arms or the right to bear the arms of families from whom they are descended. It is an independent and semi-private body of kings of arms, heralds and pursuivants responsible to the sovereign through the Earl Marshal.

Individual heraldry, as the name implies, means that an individual is granted a unique coat of arms which allude to factors such as his position in the family, ownership of fiefs, baronies or other titles, or, as happens in Spain and Portugal, his four grandparental quarterings can be marshalled together. By its very nature, individual heraldry is therefore of much help to the genealogist.

In Scotland individual heraldry is seen at its best. The high proportion of its nobility to the total population, the clan system and the relatively small number of surnames, its feudal system of land tenure and the precision of the Scottish temperament, have encouraged people to know their relative position vis-à-vis their clan chiefs. These tendencies are vividly illustrated by the large attendances at international gatherings of the clans whenever they are held. Scottish heraldry takes a rather more liberal view regarding women, who are frequently recognized as clan chieftains and lairds. This tends towards the assumption by male heirs of their mothers' surname and arms when familial succession has to pass through the female line.

Details of many coats of arms are given in Burke's *General Armory* (1884) supplemented by Cecil R. Humphery-Smith (ed.), *General Armory Two* (1973). Good outlines of British heraldry are *The Oxford Guide to Heraldry* (1988) by Thomas Woodcock (Somerset Herald) and John Martin Robinson (Maltravers Herald Extraordinary); and David Williamson, *Debrett's Guide to Heraldry and Regalia* (1994).

Grants of titles of nobility on the Continent differ greatly from the system adopted in Britain. In France families able to trace their descent to 1400 or earlier were entitled to consider themselves the equal, or peers, of the King, and were known as feudal families. Quasi-feudal families were those able to prove an uninterrupted descent coupled with the possession of a fief from before 1560, and were called gentlemen of rank, birth or blood and could assume titles at will. In England the lowest rank of the peerage is the baron, in France the écuyer or esquire. The term 'Seigneur' is the equivalent of the English Lord of the Manor, and no matter whether you were a seigneur or a duc, you owed your nobility (noblesse) to the fact that you were an écuyer. Whether you called yourself Baron, Vicomte, Comte, Marquis or Duc depended upon the number of seigneuries you owned. Thus nobility and titles depended upon the size of your property, not, as in England, on a grant by the sovereign. It was the land or 'terre' which was deemed to be a Baronie, Comté or Marquisat, not the individual who possessed it. It did not follow that the son of a Marquis was a Comte or the son of a Comte a Vicomte as in England, where an individual or family rises through the ranks of the peerage so that a member of the family of A could be ennobled as Baron B, and later becomes Viscount C, Earl of D and Duke of E. In noble English families, subsidiary titles are used by courtesy only, e.g. the Duke of Grafton, whose subsidiary titles, which may be borne by his eldest son and grandson until he inherits the dukedom, are Earl of Euston, Viscount Ipswich, and Baron Sudbury.

The use of heraldic arms in France has never been as strictly controlled as it has been in England and there is no French equivalent of the College of Arms. Arms, therefore, were not the privilege of noblemen. In 1696 Louis XIV instituted a General Armorial of France to register all coats of arms of gentlemen as well as those of ecclesiastics, burgesses and of those who enjoyed certain privileges and public rights.

In Austria and Germany since the sixteenth century the nobility has been divided into Fürsten (princes), Grafen (counts) and Freiherren (barons) which together comprise the landed class of the high nobility. The emperors tended to honour more and more families with hereditary titles to the extent that it is possible to talk of a kind of 'inflation' of titles. Much the same situation obtained in Italy, where the proliferation of small sovereign states within the Holy Roman Empire gave rise to a plethora of titled families. In Spain the titles of Vizconde, Conde, Marqués and Duque were first granted in the fourteenth century and made hereditary through primogeniture and by right of succession as in Britain. These titles, although personal, were founded either on domains that already had titles attached to them or on new lands granted by the sovereign. The right to bear arms was restricted in Navarre to the nobility. In 1595, Kings of Arms were introduced by Philip II with powers not unlike those enjoyed by their English and Scottish counterparts. The powers of this body were confirmed by law in 1951 so that arms may still be granted in Spain today much in the same way as they are in Britain.

16

MAPS

Those who are fortunate enough to find that their ancestors lived in the same town or village for generations are comparatively few. In 1973, Dr Peter Spufford, in a paper given before the Society of Genealogists, quoted from Professor Chamber's findings from the Vale of Trent, that nearly half the people died in different parishes from those in which they were born, but that a very large proportion of them, including many who died in the same parish in which they were born, lived for many years in yet other parishes. He was referring to seventeenth and eighteenth century studies. Other demographers have shown that apart from the great flow of people to London, practically all movement was restricted to a very limited distance, less than twenty miles, and a great deal of it less than ten miles. Studies in France, Italy and Hungary amongst societies of very different structure, have shown similar movements of population from as early as the fifteenth century. Of course the Industrial Revolution increased migration of this kind, especially in England, where it began earlier and continued longer.

This movement, coupled with the loss of records or their inability to show where people came from, causes many family historians to give up their research. It is at this point that real detective work is needed, and every piece of evidence must be used. Among the most useful tools at this stage are maps.

The factors inducing people to move are many, so a detailed study of local history, especially with regard to the growth of industries and the increase in enclosures, coupled with the study of local maps is now vital. County archivists are usually equipped to help you find out the history of the neighbourhood in which you are interested.

The earliest maps are those printed in the fifteenth century, but not many of these survive. Christopher Saxton's are among the earliest, followed in the seventeenth century by John Speed's maps of England and Robert Morden's in the eighteenth.

Estate maps which date from about 1570 and continue to 1860 are very useful in showing the layout of towns and villages at any given time. A series of such maps can show the progress of urban growth that accompanied the changes to many towns and villages during the Industrial Revolution.

The Enclosure Awards record the terms of enclosure and the disposition of all affected common land. An award may be accompanied by a map which surveyors drew up to show how the common land was divided, and in some cases the whole village was shown in order to delineate the property in relation to the enclosure allotment that had been claimed. Medieval enclosures of open fields, moorland and meadow have often been agreed between the Lord of the Manor and other interested parties, but there were just as many enclosures made by stealth or even by brute force. In the sixteenth and early seventeenth centuries, the Courts of Exchequer and Chancery supervised enclosures, but after 1750 they were secured by Acts of Parliament. Since 1801 general Enclosure Acts have been made to facilitate enclosures.

The Anglo-Saxon tithes of one-tenth of the produce of land, stock or industry claimed by the Church were a burden that led to disputes with farmers and landowners. The campaign to get them commuted into money payments finally resulted in the Tithe Commutation Act of 1836, and village meetings agreed on the value of tithes based on the average corn prices for the past seven years, and commissioners were appointed to award fair rents to be shared by all proprietors of land. Large-scale maps were drawn up by surveyors to show every parcel of land, path, garden, shed, outhouse, stream and factory, and apportionments set out in columns the names of owners and occupiers; description of each parcel of land; the state of cultivation and its acreage; and the tithe rent-charge. The award, map and apportionment were fastened together and sealed. Three copies were produced, one for the Parish Chest, one for the Diocesan Registry, and one for the Land Registry. In 1936 rent charges were abolished, a stock fund was created to provide compensation, and all payments were planned to terminate in 1996.

Finally, there are the Ordnance Survey maps. These are probably the most frequently used by family historians. It is of course useful to have a copy of the current series for the area in which you are interested in order to locate places as they are today, but it is the first series of these maps that show what nineteenth-century Britain looked like. This edition is the one of greatest use in establishing the whereabouts of addresses obtained from census returns and civil registration certificates.

The Ordnance Survey, or Trigonometrical Survey as it was first named, was founded in 1791, its prime object being to produce a map of Great Britain to a scale of 1 inch to the mile.

The first Ordnance Map, the 1 inch to the mile map of Kent, was in fact privately published by William Faden, but the first official Old Series maps consisted of 110 sheets, mainly 36in x 24in. This series was published between 1805 and 1873. These maps covered England and Wales, and, in terms of accuracy, are the least reliable. They should therefore be used critically. The New Series, or Second Edition, was started in 1840. There appears to have been a full-scale revision between 1893 and 1898, but all 360 sheets (12in x 18in) were published before 1899. The survey for the Third Edition began in 1901, with publication between 1903 and 1913, again comprising 360 sheets, 12in x 18in. The survey for the Fourth Edition started in 1913 and was published between 1918 and 1926. This marked a departure from its predecessors as it consisted of 146 sheets, 18in x 27in. Various revised editions have been published since the Fourth

Edition, but for the purposes of research it is only the latest series that have any obvious relevance.

Although the 1 inch to the mile maps formed the original series, larger scale maps of 6 inch and 25 inch to the mile were introduced during the second half of the nineteenth century to cover the whole of Britain. The 6 inch survey was started in 1840, and the 25 inch in 1853. In spite of considerable controversy, both from vested interests, private surveyors and on the grounds of economy, it was decided to make the 25 inch series for the whole country, except for the uncultivated districts which were to be surveyed on the 6 inch scale. From the 25 inch maps, 6 inch maps were produced by reduction. The First Edition of this series was completed between 1888 and 1893, the 25 inch maps being on sheets 38in x 25^1/₃in. The 6 inch maps published before 1881 were on sheets 36in x 24in, but thereafter they appeared in quarter sheets 18in x 12in. The first revision began in 1891 and was completed in 1914. The second revision survey began in 1904, but was drastically interrupted by the First World War. For this reason some areas were only partly revised, others not started, and the old system of revision was abandoned in 1922. Thereafter revision was confined to the 6 inch sheets, and in 1928 this was replaced by continuous revision for areas of most rapid change. As with the 1 inch series, these scales are available in the latest series.

It will be readily appreciated that the 1 inch maps are most useful for research in a fairly large area, but once the exact place of interest has been located, it is essential to use the 6 inch and 25 inch maps for the very detailed information they can provide. The choice between the two larger scales will to a great extent depend on whether the area is urban or rural.

In addition to the main series of Ordnance Survey maps there are town plans found in a variety of scales and starting at different times; the first, for St Helens, was published in 1843. The usual and current sizes are those of 50 inch to one mile, but all are worth examining for their superb workmanship and extensive detail. In some cases, even the number of seats within churches is shown.

There are of course other scales, in particular the 2^1/₂ inch series, but for research purposes the above will invariably be sufficient.

Gazetteers are an essential accompaniment to maps. For the nineteenth century, the best is *Lewis's Topographical Dictionary* (1842), which is divided into volumes covering England, Wales, Scotland and Ireland, each giving excellent details down to villages, hamlets and tithings. More recent publications are the Ordnance Survey and Bartholomew's *Gazetteers* which are adequate for use with current maps.

The British Library Map Library has one of the world's major historical collections of maps, charts, plans and topographical views, and also contains a comprehensive collection of modern maps of all countries. Similarly the copyright libraries – the National Library of Scotland, the National Library of Wales, the Bodleian Library at Oxford, Cambridge University Library and Trinity College Library, Dublin – hold extensive collections of maps, charts and plans. Indeed the best collection of Irish maps is at the library of Trinity College, Dublin. The Public Record Offices in London, Edinburgh, Belfast and Dublin, as well as the Royal Geographical Society, have their own unique and priceless collections.

County record offices have excellent collections for their own areas, including Ordnance Survey maps. In addition there are the county reference libraries, museums, and specialist societies. All these valuable and helpful sources can often be used in conjunction with other research, or specific lines of enquiry.

The Institute of Heraldic and Genealogical Studies, Northgate, Canterbury CT1 1BA, has published a very useful series of parish maps for each county of England and Wales. Each map shows the ancient parochial boundaries, the Probate Court jurisdiction affecting each area in colour, and the dates of commencement of the original registers of each parish to have survived. These maps can be obtained separately from the Institute, or bound in book form, as *The Phillinore Atlas and Index of Parish Registers* (1995).

For those interested in colonial America, several seventeenth- and eighteenth-century maps are available, but if you wish to study or plot the boundaries of original holdings in, for example, Virginia, then the most useful are the 7.5 minute series (topographic), published by the US Department of the Interior Geological Survey.

The counties of England, Wales and Scotland before and after boundary reorganization.

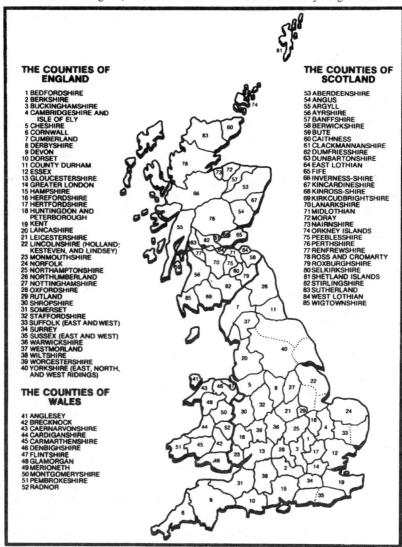

THE COUNTIES OF ENGLAND

1 BEDFORDSHIRE
2 BERKSHIRE
3 BUCKINGHAMSHIRE
4 CAMBRIDGESHIRE AND ISLE OF ELY
5 CHESHIRE
6 CORNWALL
7 CUMBERLAND
8 DERBYSHIRE
9 DEVON
10 DORSET
11 COUNTY DURHAM
12 ESSEX
13 GLOUCESTERSHIRE
14 GREATER LONDON
15 HAMPSHIRE
16 HEREFORDSHIRE
17 HERTFORDSHIRE
18 HUNTINGDON AND PETERBOROUGH
19 KENT
20 LANCASHIRE
21 LEICESTERSHIRE
22 LINCOLNSHIRE (HOLLAND; KESTEVEN, AND LINDSEY)
23 MONMOUTHSHIRE
24 NORFOLK
25 NORTHAMPTONSHIRE
26 NORTHUMBERLAND
27 NOTTINGHAMSHIRE
28 OXFORDSHIRE
29 RUTLAND
30 SHROPSHIRE
31 SOMERSET
32 STAFFORDSHIRE
33 SUFFOLK (EAST AND WEST)
34 SURREY
35 SUSSEX (EAST AND WEST)
36 WARWICKSHIRE
37 WESTMORLAND
38 WILTSHIRE
39 WORCESTERSHIRE
40 YORKSHIRE (EAST, NORTH, AND WEST RIDINGS)

THE COUNTIES OF WALES

41 ANGLESEY
42 BRECKNOCK
43 CAERNARVONSHIRE
44 CARDIGANSHIRE
45 CARMARTHENSHIRE
46 DENBIGHSHIRE
47 FLINTSHIRE
48 GLAMORGAN
49 MERIONETH
50 MONTGOMERYSHIRE
51 PEMBROKESHIRE
52 RADNOR

THE COUNTIES OF SCOTLAND

53 ABERDEENSHIRE
54 ANGUS
55 ARGYLL
56 AYRSHIRE
57 BANFFSHIRE
58 BERWICKSHIRE
59 BUTE
60 CAITHNESS
61 CLACKMANNANSHIRE
62 DUMFRIESSHIRE
63 DUNBARTONSHIRE
64 EAST LOTHIAN
65 FIFE
66 INVERNESS-SHIRE
67 KINCARDINESHIRE
68 KINROSS-SHIRE
69 KIRKCUDBRIGHTSHIRE
70 LANARKSHIRE
71 MIDLOTHIAN
72 MORAY
73 NAIRNSHIRE
74 ORKNEY ISLANDS
75 PEEBLESSHIRE
76 PERTHSHIRE
77 RENFREWSHIRE
78 ROSS AND CROMARTY
79 ROXBURGHSHIRE
80 SELKIRKSHIRE
81 SHETLAND ISLANDS
82 STIRLINGSHIRE
83 SUTHERLAND
84 WEST LOTHIAN
85 WIGTOWNSHIRE

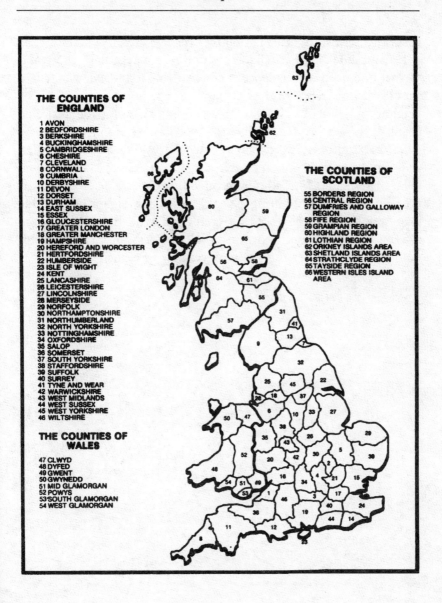

THE COUNTIES OF ENGLAND

1 AVON
2 BEDFORDSHIRE
3 BERKSHIRE
4 BUCKINGHAMSHIRE
5 CAMBRIDGESHIRE
6 CHESHIRE
7 CLEVELAND
8 CORNWALL
9 CUMBRIA
10 DERBYSHIRE
11 DEVON
12 DORSET
13 DURHAM
14 EAST SUSSEX
15 ESSEX
16 GLOUCESTERSHIRE
17 GREATER LONDON
18 GREATER MANCHESTER
19 HAMPSHIRE
20 HEREFORD AND WORCESTER
21 HERTFORDSHIRE
22 HUMBERSIDE
23 ISLE OF WIGHT
24 KENT
25 LANCASHIRE
26 LEICESTERSHIRE
27 LINCOLNSHIRE
28 MERSEYSIDE
29 NORFOLK
30 NORTHAMPTONSHIRE
31 NORTHUMBERLAND
32 NORTH YORKSHIRE
33 NOTTINGHAMSHIRE
34 OXFORDSHIRE
35 SALOP
36 SOMERSET
37 SOUTH YORKSHIRE
38 STAFFORDSHIRE
39 SUFFOLK
40 SURREY
41 TYNE AND WEAR
42 WARWICKSHIRE
43 WEST MIDLANDS
44 WEST SUSSEX
45 WEST YORKSHIRE
46 WILTSHIRE

THE COUNTIES OF WALES

47 CLWYD
48 DYFED
49 GWENT
50 GWYNEDD
51 MID GLAMORGAN
52 POWYS
53 SOUTH GLAMORGAN
54 WEST GLAMORGAN

THE COUNTIES OF SCOTLAND

55 BORDERS REGION
56 CENTRAL REGION
57 DUMFRIES AND GALLOWAY REGION
58 FIFE REGION
59 GRAMPIAN REGION
60 HIGHLAND REGION
61 LOTHIAN REGION
62 ORKNEY ISLANDS AREA
63 SHETLAND ISLANDS AREA
64 STRATHCLYDE REGION
65 TAYSIDE REGION
66 WESTERN ISLES ISLAND AREA

133

In British terms, the scale is slightly over 2½ inch to the mile.

If your line of research peters out in a particular place, and further documentary evidence is not available to indicate where you should search next, you will have to examine the records of neighbouring parishes in an ever-increasing circle for the next clue or link, to enable you to find the evidence you are seeking. As Gerald Hamilton-Edwards has pointed out: 'Villagers would often walk up the road in search of refreshment and change, and many a village lad met his future bride through first contacting her father or brother in the neighbouring "local".' With the higher classes this may well be the neighbouring county, but as these people are usually better documented, the problem does not so often arise until one gets back to the sixteenth century or earlier.

17

THE PROFESSIONAL
APPROACH

It has to be admitted at the outset that genealogy is a hobby, and that those who undertake to trace their ancestors want to do it for themselves. It is, however, equally true that often this is impossible. If you trace your ancestry to some part of the country remote from that in which you live, or if you are an American or Australian wanting to trace the origin of your emigrant ancestors, it becomes necessary sometimes to seek professional help.

Ancestry research is also a time-consuming and complex business and many researchers employ professional genealogists or record agents to help them on their way. Depending on the particular research needed, you may need a specific local expert or a company who can co-ordinate research in a wide geographical area. For over 200 years, Debrett have chronicled the families of the aristocracy but Debrett Ancestry Research Ltd now researches families from all walks of life in Britain, Ireland, North America, Australia and New Zealand. There are several advantages in using a reputable company rather than an individual researcher: the company calls upon the services of specialists in many different fields and locations;

where companies use freelance researchers they will monitor the quality of the results; and a high standard of work, service and presentation can be expected.

For those wishing to employ an individual searcher, *Family Tree Magazine*, published monthly and widely available in newsagents, carries advertisements from professional researchers as well as a good deal of helpful advice. *The Genealogical Services Directory* (published annually, available for £5.00 from G. R. Specialist Information Services, 33 Nursery Road, Nether Poppleton, York YO2 6NN) advertizes a wide variety of services for family historians including research. Of course, neither of these sources has any 'vetting' procedure for those who advertize with them. The Association of Genealogists and Record Agents (AGRA), founded in 1968, is an organization of professional researchers in the United Kingdom and Ireland with a code of practice. In general, a genealogist directs the research while a record agent undertakes it. A list of AGRA members is available at a cost of £2.00 from The Secretaries, 29 Badgers Close, Horsham, West Sussex RH12 5RU.

Whether you employ a company or an individual, it is important to remember that fees are based on the time spent on research, not on results, which can never be predicted with any precision. It is also important to supply the professional with all the relevant information, distinguishing between what is certain and what is only traditional, thus ensuring that they do not have to spend time establishing facts you knew already.

Family Tree magazine has published in various issues articles entitled 'Indexers and their Indexes'. These cover a large number of subjects and professions.

APPENDIX I:
USEFUL DATES

It is important to be aware of certain dates when searching documents in which to look for information. The following is a list of some of those most useful to genealogists.

1509 HENRY VIII
1522 Earliest known Muster Roll
1538 Parish registers ordered to be kept
1542 Administrative Union of Wales with England
1547 EDWARD VI
1552 Ulster King of Arms established
1553 MARY I
1558 ELIZABETH I
1558 Chancery Proceedings C.2 & C.3 Indexes begin
1567 Earliest Huguenot & Walloon registers
1574 Colonial State Papers published. Continued to 1738
1597 Bishops' Transcripts begin
1600 Memoirs of officers of the Royal Navy first kept
1601 Poor Relief Act

1601 East India Company founded
1603 JAMES I and VI of Scotland
1626 CHARLES I
1642 Civil wars interrupt parish register keeping
1644 Earliest Presbyterian registers
1644 Earliest Independent (Congregational) registers
1645 Inquisitions *post mortem* end
1647 Earliest Baptist registers
1649 COMMONWEALTH
1649 CHARLES II, but in exile
1650s Earliest Quaker registers
1653 Provincial probate courts abolished
1660 CHARLES II – the Restoration
1660 Provincial probate courts re-established
1660 Parish registers resumed
1662 Poor Relief Act
1662 Hearth Tax
1663 Earliest Roman Catholic registers
1667 Burial in woollen begins
1669 Earliest Lutheran registers
1670 Earliest Synagogue registers – Bevis Marks
1677 Lee's Collection of Names of Merchants in London
1679 Burial in woollen more strictly enforced
1684 Huguenot registers begin in London
1685 JAMES II
1688 Hearth Tax abolished
1689 WILLIAM and MARY
1689 Toleration Act for Protestant Nonconformists
1689 Earliest Royal Dutch Chapel registers
1690 Great Synagogue founded in London
1695 Dissenters' lists of births in parish registers
1698 Duties payable on entries in parish registers
1702 ANNE
1703 Repeat of duties on entries in parish registers
1708 Earliest Artillery Muster Rolls
1710 Tax on apprentice indentures
1714 GEORGE I

1714 Chancery proceedings filed under six clerks
1727 GEORGE II
1732 Earliest Cavalry and Infantry Muster Rolls
1733 Abolition of Latin in legal documents
1738 Earliest Calvinistic Methodist registers
1741 Earliest Moravian registers
1741 Earliest Scotch Church registers
1752 Gregorian Calendar introduced in Britain
1752 Earliest Lady Huntingdon's New Connexion registers
1753 Earliest Inghamite registers
1754 Lord Hardwicke's Marriage Act
1754 First printed annual Army Lists
1760 GEORGE III
1762 Earliest Unitarian registers
1762 Earliest Swiss Church registers
1772 First Navy Lists
1779 Earliest New Connexion Methodist registers
1780 Earliest Wesleyan registers
1780 Male Servants Tax
1783 Duty on parish register entries
1784 New South Wales original correspondence C.O.201
1787 Earliest Swedenborgian registers
1794 Abolition of parish register duties
1800 Royal College of Surgeons founded
1800 Earliest Bible Christian registers
1806 Earliest Primitive Methodist registers
1813 Rose's Act – new parish register books
1814 Cape Colony C.O.48
1814 Pigot's Commercial Directory
1820 GEORGE IV
1823 New laws concerning marriage by licence
1823 Scottish testaments prior to 1823 transferred to Scottish
      Records Office
1829 Earliest Irvingite registers
1830 WILLIAM IV
1835 Earliest Universalist registers
1837 VICTORIA

1837	Civil registration in England and Wales
1841	Census 7 June
1842	Civil registration in Channel Islands
1845	Kelly's Directories
1845	Registration of Protestant marriages in Ireland
1849	Civil registration of births in Isle of Man
1851	Census 30 March
1855	Civil registration in Scotland
1858	Central probate registry
1861	Census 7 April
1864	Civil registration in Ireland
1864	Civil registration of marriages in Isle of Man
1871	Census 2 April
1872	Penalties for failing to register births, marriages and deaths
1876	Civil registration of deaths in Isle of Man
1881	Census 3 April
1891	Census 5 April
1901	EDWARD VII
1901	Census 31 March – open to public search after 2001
1910	GEORGE V
1916	Rebellion in Ireland
1922	Partition of Ireland and destruction of Four Courts
1927	Adoption registration – records kept at ONS
1937	EDWARD VIII
1937	GEORGE VI
1943	Ulster King of Arms transferred to Dublin
1952	ELIZABETH II
1975	Children's Act – amends previous Adoption Acts

Appendix II:
A Checklist of
Genealogical
Sources

Group I–Private Records, Papers and Relics

1 Family Bible
2 Family pedigree or other written account, notes or memoranda by members of the family concerning its history and traditions
3 Diaries
4 Notebooks about family events
5 Birthday books
6 Account books
7 Stock, share and tontine (annuity) certificates
8 Deeds relating to property, including estate maps
9 Marriage contracts and settlements
10 Baptismal certificates and other records
11 Barmitzvah cards
12 Confirmation and first communion certificates
13 Funeral cards
14 Bank books, life assurance policies

15 School and university records, certificates and prizes
16 Degrees
17 Certificates of ordination
18 Driving and similar licences
19 Passports, identity cards, denizations, naturalizations
20 Testimonials
21 Sporting prizes and cups
22 Letters
23 Bookplates
24 Club and professional association membership records
25 Trade union records
26 Armed service records
27 Medals and decorations
28 Civic awards
29 Samplers
30 Mourning and signet rings, seals and fobs
31 Crested or armorial silver, glass and china
32 Portraits and photographs
33 Records of changes of name
34 Divorce proceedings and settlements
35 Medical certificates and records

GROUP II–PUBLIC RECORDS

36 Wills
37 Marriage proclamations (banns) and licences
38 Marriage certificates and bonds
39 Birth certificates
40 Death certificates
41 Burial records, receipts for mort cloths, leasehold and freehold records of burial plots, cremation certificates, graveyard and cemetery records, monumental inscriptions
42 Apprenticeship indentures
43 East India Company records
44 Family lawyers' records
45 Hatchments, paintings and engravings or armorial bearings
46 Certificates of grants of arms

47   Records of lawsuits concerning intestacies and illegitimacies
48   Adoption records
49   Documents relating to criminal conviction and transportation
50   Patents for inventions
51   Grants and patents of land and feet of fines
52   Master mariners' certificates and the like
53   Notarial records
54   Census records
55   Parish registers
56   Bishops' and archdeacons' transcripts
57   Inquisitions *post mortem*
58   Royalist composition papers
59   Protestation returns and oaths of allegiance
60   Records of the court of law

GROUP III–MISCELLANEOUS RECORDS AND INDEXES

61   Obituaries
62   Names of houses, estates and plantations associated with the family
63   Local and national newspapers and journals; press cuttings
64   Biographies and autobiographies
65   Local and national directories
66   Publications – books, articles, poems, etc.
67   Genealogical guides and reference books
68   International Genealogical Index (IGI) (Mormon Genealogical Collections)
69   National Pedigree Index (Society of Genealogists) Directories of members' interests published by UK family history and genealogical societies
70   Collections of deposited pedigrees at Society of Genealogists, county record offices, libraries, etc.
71   Catalogue of British Library printed books (reference to family histories or biographies) and MS collections
72   Topographical dictionaries
73   Titles of unpublished theses submitted to British universities

APPENDIX III:
USEFUL ADDRESSES

Before carrying out research, it is important to know where to find records, because these are not necessarily in the obvious place, the local county record office. The general principles about the whereabouts of archives need to be understood, in the first place. Church records in England and Wales are organized by dioceses which are not always the same as counties, although the majority of county record offices are in fact diocesan record offices as well. These are of primary importance since as well as parish registers and bishops' transcripts, wills were proved in Church courts, and so are in diocesan archives. The records of the central government, including the armed forces, national courts, taxation, and the superior probate court, are in the Public Record Office, while records of local administration like county quarter session courts are in county record offices. Many landowners deposited their estate records in county record offices, but it is important to appreciate that some of these people owned property in several counties, and generally their archives will be in the county where they lived, rather than the more obvious county where the land was. Another complication is

145

the creation of new counties in 1974, which is confusing, as earlier records tend to be kept according to the old counties. The maps on pages 132 and 133 show the old and new boundaries, and the list below is cross-referenced according to this. Repositories are listed on the following pages according to the old counties.

It is important to remember that many church records are still held in the churches and chapels, in the custody of the respective clergymen, particularly in Ireland. Access to these records is not an automatic right for researchers, and their custodians have more important duties than accommodating family historians, who should remember the courtesies of both a prior appointment and a donation to church funds.

It is important to contact the repository before you visit, to find out whether they have the records you require, their opening hours, any special regulations, and whether you have to book a fiche reader or desk. Many county record offices require you to have a County Archive Research Network (CARN) reader's ticket, but the PRO and British Library operate their own systems. You will need to take with you proof of your identity and address, paper and pencil – you will usually not be allowed to use a pen. Smoking, eating and drinking are not allowed (although there is often an area where you can eat food you have brought with you), and you should avoid taking children or companions who are not helping with the research, as there is little space for visitors and few facilities. Conversation should be kept to a minimum, cameras, mobile phones and tape recorders are not usually allowed, and you should check before taking a laptop computer. For more details about repositories and their use, see Gibson and Peskett, *Record Offices and How to Find Them* (FFHS 1998) and *The Genealogical Services Directory* (GR Specialist Information Services, York YO2 6NN). These are invaluable and list smaller and more specialized archives.

Manorial Records and other Landowners' Archives
There is no published guide but the Historical Manuscripts Commission maintains the Manorial Documents Register and the National Register of Archives, which list the whereabouts of such

material where it is known. The indexes and catalogues may be consulted at Quality House, Quality Court, Chancery Lane, London WC2A 1HP. Website: http://www.hmc.gov.uk/main.htm.

ENGLAND

London and General

Baptist Union Library, PO Box 44, 129 The Broadway, Didcot, Oxon OX11 8RT   Tel 01235 512077

The British Library, 96 Euston Road, London NW1 2DB
Tel 0171 412 7626

Census Division, ONS Segensworth Rd, Titchfield PO15 5RR

College of Arms, Queen Victoria Street, London EC4V 4BT
Tel 0171 248 2762, fax 0171 248 6448

Debrett Ancestry Research Ltd, PO Box 7, Alresford, Hants
SO24 9EN   Tel 01962 732676, fax 01962 734040
Website:http://www.debrettancestry.demon.co.uk

Dr Williams's Library, 14 Gordon Square, London WC1H 0AG
Tel 0171 387 3727, fax 0171 388 1142

Family Records Centre (ONS and PRO), 1 Myddelton Street,
London EC1R 1UW   Tel 0181 392 5300, fax 0181 392 5307
Website: http://www.pro.gov.uk and www.ons.gov.uk. The Family
Search collection of databases is also available here, including the
IGI, LDS Ancestral Files, LDS Family History Library
Catalogue, index to Scottish church records, and US Social
Security death indexes

Federation of Family History Societies, c/o The Benson Room,
Birmingham & Midland Institute, Margaret Street, Birmingham
B3 3BS

Genealogical Libraries of the Church of Jesus Christ of Latter-Day Saints, Hyde Park Family History Centre, Church of Jesus Christ of Latter-Day Saints, 64–8 Exhibition Road, London SW7 2PA

General Register Office, Smedley Hydro, Birkdale, Southport PR8 2HH (postal searches)   Tel 0151 471 4800

Guildhall Library, Aldermanbury, London EC2P 2EJ Tel 0171 332 1863, fax 0171 600 3384

The Guild of One-Name Studies, Box G, 14 Charterhouse Buildings, Goswell Road, London EC1M 7BA

House of Lords Record Office, House of Lords, London SW1A 0PW   Tel 0171 219 3074

Huguenot Library, University College, Gower Street, London WC1E 6BP   Tel 0171 380 7094

John Rylands Library, University of Manchester, Deansgate, Manchester M3 3EH   Tel 0161 834 5343

London Metropolitan Archives, 40 Northampton Road, London EC1R 0HB   Tel 0171 332 3820, fax 0171 833 9136

Ministry of Defence CS(R)2b, Bourne Avenue, Hayes, Middlesex UB3 1RS (post-1914 army and navy records)   Tel 0181 573 3831

NORCAP (National Organisation for Counselling Adoptees and Parents), 112 Church Road, Wheatley OX33 1LU. Tel 01865 875000, fax 01865 875686

Oriental and India Office Collections, The British Library, 96 Euston Road, London NW1 2DB   Tel 0171 412 7873

Principal Probate Registry, First Avenue House, 42–48 High Holborn, London WC1V 6NP   Tel 0171 936 7000

The Principal Registry of the Family Division, First Avenue House, High Holborn, London WC2R 1LP   Tel 0171 842 7574

Public Record Office, Ruskin Avenue, Kew, Surrey TW9 4DU Tel 0181 876 3444, fax 0181 878 8905

RAF Personnel Management Centre, RAF Innsworth, Gloucester GL3 1EZ   Tel 01452 712612 ex 7906

Royal Commission on Historical Manuscripts, Quality House, Quality Court, Chancery Lane, London WC2A 1HP Tel 0171 242 1198, fax 0171 831 3550

Society of Friends (Quakers) Library, Friends House, Euston Road, London NW1 2BJ   Tel 0171 663 1135, fax 0171 663 1001

Society of Genealogists, 14 Charterhouse Buildings, Goswell Road, London EC1M 7BA   Tel 0171 251 8799

Unitarian Association, Essex Hall, Essex Street, Strand, London WC2

United Reformed Church History Society, 86 Tavistock Place, London WC1H 9RT   Tel 0171 837 7661

Bedfordshire

Bedfordshire Record Office, County Hall, Bedford MK42 9AP Tel 01234 228833/228777/363222, fax 01234 228854

Berkshire (see also Buckinghamshire; Oxfordshire)

Berkshire Record Office, Shire Hall, Shinfield Park, Reading RG2 9XD   Tel 0118 901 5132, fax 0118 901 5131

Buckinghamshire (see also Berkshire)

Buckinghamshire Record Office, County Hall, Aylesbury HP20 1UV   Tel 01296 382587, fax 01296 382405

Cambridgeshire

Cambridgeshire County Record Office, Shire Hall, Castle Hill, Cambridge CB3 0AP   Tel 01223 717281, fax 01223 717201

Cheshire (see also Derbyshire; Greater Manchester)

Cheshire Record Office, Duke Street, Chester CH1 1RL
Tel 01244 602574, fax 01244 603812

Chester Archives, Town Hall, Chester CH1 2HJ
Tel 01244 402110, fax 01244 312243

Stockport Archive Service, Central Library, Wellington Road South, Stockport SK1 3RS   Tel 0161 474 4530, fax 0161 474 7750

Wirral Archives Service, Birkenhead Reference Library, Borough Road, Birkenhead L41 2XB   Tel 0151 652 6106, fax 0151 653 7320

Cornwall

Cornwall Record Office, County Hall, Truro TR1 3AY
Tel 01872 273698/232127, fax 01872 270340

Cumberland (now part of Cumbria)

Cumbria (includes Cumberland, Westmorland, parts of Lancashire and Yorkshire)

Cumbria Record Office, The Castle, Carlisle CA3 8UR
Tel 01228 607284, fax 01228 607274

Whitehaven Local Studies Library, Scotch Street, Whitehaven CA28 7NJ   Tel 01946 852920, fax 01946 852919

Derbyshire

Derbyshire Record Office, County Offices, Matlock DE4 3AG
Tel 01629 585347, fax 01629 57611

Devon

Devon Record Office, Castle Street, Exeter EX4 3PU
Tel 01392 384253, fax 01392 384256

Plymouth and West Devon Record Office, Unit 3, Clare Place,
Coxside, Plymouth PL4 0JW   Tel 01752 305940, fax 01752 223939

Dorset (see also Hampshire)

Dorset Record Office, Bridport Road, Dorchester DT1 1RP
Tel 01305 250550, fax 03105 257184

Durham (see also Cleveland; Tyne and Wear; Yorkshire)

Durham County Record Office, County Hall, Durham DH1 5UL
Tel 0191 383 3253/3474, fax 0191 383 4500

Durham University Library Archives and Special Collections,
Palace Green Section, Palace Green, Durham DH1 3RN
Tel 0191 374 3001, fax 0191 374 7481

Essex (see also Greater London)

Essex Record Office, Colchester and North-East Essex Branch,
Stanwell House, Stanwell Street, Colchester CO2 7DL
Tel 01206 572099, fax 01206 574541

Essex Record Office, County Hall, Chelmsford CM1 1LX
Tel 01245 430067/8, fax 01245 430085

Essex Record Office, Southend Branch, Central Library, Victoria
Avenue, Southend-on-Sea SS2 6EX   Tel 01702 612621, fax 01702
464253

Gloucestershire

Bristol Record Office, 'B' Bond Warehouse, Smeaton Road,
Bristol BS1 6XN   Tel 0117 922 5692, fax 0117 922 4236

Gloucestershire Record Office, Clarence Row, off Alvin Street, Gloucester GL1 3DW   Tel 01452 425295, fax 01452 426378

Hampshire and Isle of Wight

Hampshire Record Office, Sussex Street, Winchester SO23 8TH Tel 01962 846154, fax 01962 878681

Portsmouth City Records Office, 3 Museum Road, Portsmouth PO1 2LJ   Tel 01705 827261, fax 01705 875276

Southampton Archives Service, Civic Centre, Southampton SO9 4XR   Tel 01703 832251/223855 ex 2251

Isle of Wight County Record Office, 26 Hillside, Newport, IoW PO30 2EB   Tel/fax 01983 823820/1

Herefordshire

Hereford Record Office, The Old Barracks, Harold Street, Hereford HR1 2QX   Tel 01432 265441, fax 01432 370248

Hertfordshire (see also Greater London)

Hertfordshire Record Office, County Hall, Hertford SG13 8JE Tel 01992 555105, fax 01992 555113

Huntingdonshire

Cambridgeshire County Record Office (Huntingdon), Grammar School Walk, Huntingdon PE18 6LF   Tel 01480 375842, fax 01480 459563

Kent (see also Greater London)

Canterbury City and Cathedral Archives, The Precincts, Canterbury CT1 2EH   Tel 01227 463510, fax 01227 762897

Centre for Kentish Studies, County Hall, Maidstone ME14 1XQ
Tel 01622 694363, fax 01622 694379

East Kent Archives Centre, Enterprise Business Park, Honeywood
Road, Whitfield, Dover CT16 3HS

Medway Archives and Local Studies Centre, Civic Centre, Strood
ME2 4AW   Tel 01634 732714, fax 01634 297060

Lancashire

Bolton Archive and Local Studies Service, Central Library,
Le Mans Crescent, Bolton BL1 1SE   Tel 01204 522311,
fax 01294 363224

Bury Archive Service, Edwin Street, Bury BL9 0AS
Tel 0161 797 6697

Cumbria Record Office, 140 Duke Street, Barrow-in-Furness
LA14 1XW   Tel 01229 894363, fax 01229 894371

Greater Manchester County Record Office, 56 Marshall Street,
New Cross, Manchester M4 5FU   Tel 0161 832 5284,
fax 0161 839 3808

John Rylands University Library of Manchester, 150 Deansgate,
Manchester M3 3EH   Tel 0161 834 5343, fax 0161 834 5574

Lancashire Record Office, Bow Lane, Preston PR1 2RE
Tel 01772 263039, fax 01772 263050

Liverpool Record Office, City Library, William Brown Street,
Liverpool L3 8EW   Tel 0151 225 5417, fax 0151 207 1342

Manchester Central Library, Local Studies Unit, St Peter's Square,
Manchester M2 5PD   Tel 0161 234 1980, fax 0161 234 1927

Rochdale Local Studies Library, Central Library, The Esplanade,
Rochdale OO16 1AQ   Tel 01706 864915

Salford Archives Centre, 658/662 Liverpool Road, Irlam,
Manchester M44 5AD   Tel 0161 775 5643

Tameside Archive Service, Local Studies Library, Astley
Cheetham Public Library, Trinity Street, Stalybridge SK15 2BN
Tel 0161 338 2708, fax 0161 303 8289

Wigan Record Office, Town Hall, Leigh WN7 2DY
Tel 01942 404430, fax 01942 404505

Leicestershire and Rutland

Leicestershire Record Office, Long Street, Wigston Magna,
Leicester LE18 2AH   Tel 0116 257 1080, fax 0116 257 1120

Lincolnshire (see also Humberside)

Lincolnshire Archives Office, St Rumbold Street, Lincoln LN5 5AB
Tel 01582 526204, fax 01522 530047

North East Lincolnshire Archives, Town Hall, Town Hall Square,
Grimsby DN31 1HX   Tel 01472 323585

Norfolk

Norfolk Record Office, Gildengate House, Anglia Square, Upper
Green Lane, Norwich NR3 1AX   Tel 01603 761349,
fax 01603 761885

Northamptonshire

Northamptonshire Record Office, Wootton Hall Park,
Northampton NN4 8BQ   Tel 01604 762129, fax 01604 767562

Northumberland

Berwick upon Tweed Record Office, Council Offices, Wallace
Green, Berwick upon Tweed TD15 1ED   Tel 01289 330044,
fax 01289 330540

Morpeth Records Centre, The Kylins, Loansdean, Morpeth NE61 2EQ   Tel 01670 504084, fax 01670 514815

Northumberland Record Office, Melton Park, North Gosforth, Newcastle upon Tyne NE3 5QX   Tel 0191 236 2680, fax 0191 217 0905

Tyne and Wear Archives Service, Blandford House, Blandford Square, Newcastle upon Tyne NE1 4JA   Tel 0191 232 6789, fax 0191 230 2614

Nottinghamshire (see also Yorkshire)

Nottinghamshire Archives, County House, Castle Meadow Road, Nottingham NG2 1AG   Tel 0115 958 1634, fax 0115 958 3997

Oxfordshire

Bodleian Library, Department of Western Manuscripts, Oxford OX1 3BG   Tel 01865 277152, fax 01865 277187

Centre for Oxfordshire Studies, Central Library, Westgate, Oxford OX1 1DJ   Tel 01865 815749

Oxfordshire County Record Office, County Hall, New Road, Oxford OX1 1ND   Tel 01865 815203

Rutland (see Leicestershire)

Shropshire and Salop

Shropshire Records and Research Centre, Castle Gates, Shrewsbury SY2 2AQ   Tel 01743 255350, fax 01743 255355

Somerset

Bath and North East Somerset Record Office, Guildhall, Bath BA1 5AW   Tel 01225 477421

Somerset Record Office, Obridge Road, Taunton TA2 7PU
Tel 01823 337600, fax 01823 325402

Staffordshire

Dudley Archives and Local History Service, Mount Pleasant
Street, Coseley, Dudley WV14 9JR   Tel/fax 01384 812770

Lichfield Record Office, The Friary, Lichfield WS13 6QG
Tel 01543 510720, fax 01543 411138

Staffordshire Record Office, County Buildings, Eastgate Street,
Stafford ST16 2LZ   Tel 01785 278373, fax 01785 178384

Walsall Archives Service, Local History Centre, Essex Street,
Walsall WS2 7AS   Tel 01922 721305/6, fax 01922 634954

William Salt Library, Eastgate Street, Stafford ST16 2LZ
Tel 01785 278372

Wolverhampton Archives and Local Studies, 42–50 Snow Hill,
Wolverhampton WV2 4AG   Tel 01902 552480, fax 01902 552481

Suffolk

Suffolk Record Office, Central Library, Clapham Road, Lowestoft
NR32 1DR   Tel 01502 405357, fax 01502 405350

Suffolk Record Office, Gatacre Road, Ipswich IP1 2LQ
Tel 01473 584541, fax 01473 584533

Suffolk Record Office, Raingate Street, Bury St Edmunds IP33 2AR
Tel 01284 352352, fax 01284 352355

Surrey

Surrey History Centre, 130 Goldsworth Road, Woking GU21 1ND
Tel 01483 594594, fax 01483 594595

Sussex

East Sussex Record Office, The Maltings, Castle Precincts, Lewes BN7 1YT   Tel 01243 533911, fax 01243 777979

West Sussex Record Office, Sherburne House, 3 Orchard Street, Chichester PO19 1RN   Tel 01243 533911, fax 01243 777979

Warwickshire

Birmingham City Archives, Birmingham Central Library, Chamberlain Square, Birmingham B3 3HQ   Tel 0121 303 4217, fax 0121 212 9397

Coventry City Record Office, Mandela House, Bayley Lane, Coventry CV1 5RG   Tel 01203 832418, fax 01203 832421

Warwick County Record Office, Priory Park, Cape Road, Warwick CV34 4JS   Tel 01926 412735, fax 01826 412509

Westmorland (now part of Cumbria)

Cumbria Record Office, County Offices, Kendal LA9 4RQ Tel 01539 773540, fax 01539 773439

Isle of Wight (see also Hampshire)

Isle of Wight County Record Office, 26 Hillside, Newport PO30 2EB Tel/fax 01983 823820/1

Wiltshire

Wiltshire Record Office, County Hall, Trowbridge BA14 8JG Tel 01225 713139, fax 01225 713715

Worcestershire

Worcestershire Record Office, County Hall, Spetchley Road, Worcester WR5 2NP   Tel 01905 766351, fax 01905 763000

Yorkshire

Barnsley Archive and Local Studies Dept, Central Library, Shambles Street, Barnsley S70 2JF   Tel 01226 773950, fax 01226 773955

Borthwick Institute of Historical Research, University of York, St Anthony's Hall, Peasholme Green, York YO1 2PW Tel 01904 642315, fax 01904 633284

Bradford District Archives, 15 Canal Road, Bradford BD1 4AT Tel 01274 731931, fax 01274 734013

Calderdale District Archives, Calderdale Central Library, Northgate, Halifax HX1 1UN   Tel 01422 392636, fax 01422 341083

Doncaster Archives Dept, King Edward Street, Balby, Doncaster DN4 0NA
Tel 01302 859811

East Riding of Yorkshire Archive Office, County Hall, Champney Road, Beverley HU17 9BA   Tel 01482 885007, fax 01482 885463

Kirklees District Archives, Huddersfield Central Library, Princess Alexandra Walk, Huddersfield HD1 2SU   Tel 01484 221966, fax 01484 518361

Leeds District Archives, Chapeltown Road, Sheepscar, Leeds LS7 3AP   Tel 0113 262 8339, fax 0113 262 4707

North Yorkshire County Record Office, Malpas Road, Northallerton, North Yorkshire DL7 8AF   Tel 01609 777585, fax 01609 777078

Rotherham Archives and Local Studies Section, Brian O'Malley Central Library, Walker Place, Rotherham S65 1JH

Tel 01709 823616, fax 01709 823650

Sheffield Archives, 52 Shoreham Street, Sheffield S1 4SP
Tel 0114 273 4756, fax 0114 273 5009

Teeside Archives, Exchange House, 6 Marton Road,
Middlesbrough TS1 1DB   Tel 01642 248321

West Yorkshire Archive Service and Registry of Deeds, Newstead
Road, Wakefield WF1 2DT   Tel 01924 305980, fax 01924 305983

York City Archives Dept, Art Gallery Building, Exhibition
Square, York YO1 2EW   Tel 01904 551878, fax 01904 551877

WALES

Wales now includes the former county of Monmouthshire, which
was formerly part of England. Until recent years the National
Library of Wales, Aberystwyth, was the principal repository, and the
only one authorized for Church records. Although local record
offices have now been established, the National Library remains
predominant, and *inter alia* holds all probate records and bishops'
transcripts. Welsh counties have also been reorganized; the former
counties of Cardigan, Carmarthen and Pembroke now form the
single county of Dyfed; the former county of Glamorgan, together
with small parts of Brecon and Monmouth, forms the three new
counties of West, Mid and South Glamorgan which are served by a
single record office; the remainder of Monmouthshire is now called
Gwent; the remainder of Breconshire, with Radnorshire and Montgomeryshire, forms the new county of Powys; Flintshire, most of
Denbighshire, and a small part of Merioneth form the new county of
Clwyd; and finally Anglesey, Caernarvonshire, the remainder of
Merioneth and a small part of Denbighshire form the new county of
Gwynedd.

National Library of Wales, Dept of Manuscripts and Records,
Penglais, Aberystwyth, Dyfed SY23 3BU   Tel 01970 623816,
fax 01970 625713

Anglesey

Anglesey Record Office, Shire Hall, Glanhwfa Road, Llangefni, Gwynedd LL77 7TW   Tel 01248 752080

Caernarvonshire

Caernarfon Record Office, Victoria Dock, Caernarfon, Gwynedd LL55 1TB   Tel 01286 679095, fax 01286 679637

Dept of Manuscripts, Main Library, University College of North Wales, Bangor, Gwynedd LL57 2DG   Tel 01248 351151, fax 01248 370576

Cardiganshire

Cardiganshire Archives, County Offices, Marine Terrace, Aberystwyth SY23 2DE   Tel 01970 633697/8

National Library of Wales, see above

Carmarthenshire

Carmarthenshire Archives Service, County Hall, Carmarthen SA31 1JP   Tel 01267 224184, fax 01267 230848

Denbighshire

Denbighshire Record Office, 46 Clwyd Street, Ruthin LL15 1HP Tel 01824 703077, fax 01824 705180

Flintshire

Flintshire Record Office, The Old Rectory, Hawarden, Deeside CH5 3NR   Tel 01244 532364, fax 01244 538344

Glamorgan

Glamorgan Record Office, The Glamorgan Building, King Edward VII Avenue, Cathays Park, Cardiff CF1 3NE

Tel 01222 780282, fax 01222 780284

West Glamorgan Archive Service, County Hall, Oystermouth
Road, Swansea SA1 3NS   Tel 01792 636589, fax 01792 637130

Merioneth

Merioneth Archives, Cae Penarlag, Dolgellau, Gwynedd LL40 2YB
Tel 01341 424444, fax 01341 424505

Monmouthshire

Gwent Record Office, County Hall, Cwmbran, Gwent NP44 2XH
Tel 01633 644886, fax 01633 648382

Pembrokeshire

Pembrokeshire Record Office, The Castle, Haverfordwest, Dyfed
SA61 2EF   Tel 01437 763707

Powys (Brecknock, Montgomeryshire, Radnorshire)

Powys County Archives Office, County Hall, Llandridnod Wells,
Powys LD1 5LG   Tel 01597 826008, fax 01597 827162

SCOTLAND

Although regional and other archives have been formed recently
outside Edinburgh, in general these hold specialized material which
will be needed only when that in Edinburgh has been exhausted.

General Register Office for Scotland (birth, marriage and death
certificates, censuses, parish registers), New Register House,
Princes Street, Edinburgh EH1 3YT   Tel 0131 334 0380,
fax 0131 314 4400

National Archives of Scotland (the Scottish Record Office), HM
General Register House, Princes Street, Edinburgh EH1 3YH

Tel 0131 535 1314, fax 0131 535 1360

West Register House, Charlotte Square, Edinburgh EH2 4DF

IRELAND
(including Northern Ireland and the Republic of Ireland)

Although Northern Ireland (part of the United Kingdom) and the Republic of Ireland (Eire) have been politically separate from 1922, their former union means that their archives are not separate. In particular many archives relating to Northern Ireland are in the Republic, and the reverse applies to a lesser extent.

The Genealogical Office, 2 Kildare Street, Dublin 2
Tel +3531 618811

The General Registrar Office for Ireland, Joyce House,
8–11 Lombard Street East, Dublin 2   Tel +3531 6711000

General Register Office for Northern Ireland, Oxford House,
49–55 Chichester Street, Belfast BT1 4HL
Tel 01232 235211/252044/252120

National Archives, Bishop Street, Dublin 8   Tel +3531 4072300

National Library of Ireland, Kildare Street, Dublin 2
Tel +3531 6030200

Public Record Office for Northern Ireland, 66 Balmoral Avenue,
Belfast BT9 6NY   Tel 01232 251318, fax 01232 255999

Registry of Deeds, King's Inn, Henrietta Street, Dublin 1
Tel +3531 6707500

THE ISLE OF MAN

Civil Registry, Registries Building, Deemsters Walk, Bucks Road,
Douglas IM1 3AR   Tel: 01624 687039, fax 01624 687004

Manx National Heritage Library, Manx Museum, Kingswood Grove, Douglas IM1 3LY

THE CHANNEL ISLANDS

Guernsey

The Greffe, Royal Court House, St Peter Port, GY1 2PD
Tel 01481 725277

Island Archives Service, 29 Victoria Road, St Peter Port, GY1 HU
Tel 01481 724512

Priaulx Library, Candie Road, St Peter Port GY1 1UG
Tel 01481 721998

Jersey

Jersey Archives Service, Jersey Museum, The Weybridge, St Helier
JE2 3NF   Tel 01534 617441

Judicial Greffe, Westway Chambers, Don Street, St Helier JE2 4TR
Tel 01534 502300

Société Jersiaise, 9 Pier Road, St Helier JE2 4UW
Tel 01534 30538

Superintendent Registrar, 10 Royal Square, St Helier, Jersey
JE2 4WA

APPENDIX IV:
RECOMMENDED
READING

GENERAL

Angus Baxter, *In Search of Your European Roots* (Genealogical Publishing Co. Inc., Baltimore 1985)

Amanda Bevan (ed.), *Tracing Your Ancestors in the Public Record Office* (PRO 1999)

Burke's Family Index (Burke's Peerage 1976)

Jane Cox, Stella Colwell, *Never Been Here Before? A Genealogist's Guide to the Family Records Centre* (PRO 1997)

Family Tree Magazine (monthly), 61 Great Whyte, Ramsey PE17 1HL: this provides a postal book service

Federation of Family History Societies publications: various subjects

Terrick Fitzhugh, *The Dictionary of Genealogy* (Alphabooks 1985)

J. Gibson, *Gibson Genealogical Guides*, various subjects (FFHS)

J. Gibson and E. Hampson, *Marriage, Census, and Other Indexes for Family Historians* (FFHS 1998)

——, *Specialist Indexes for Family Historians* (FFHS 1998)

J. Gibson and P. Peskett, *Record Offices and How to Find Them* (FFHS 1998)

David Hey, *The Oxford Companion to Local and Family History* (OUP 1996)

George W. Marshall, *The Genealogist's Guide* (Genealogical Publishing Company 1967)

My Ancestors Were . . . series (Society of Genealogists)

PRO publications: see PRO website (http://www.pro.gov.uk) for full catalogue

Colin D. Rogers, *Tracing Missing Persons* (Manchester University Press 1983)

David Shorney, *Protestant Nonconformity and Roman Catholicism* (PRO 1996)

E. Silverthorne (ed.), *London Local Archives* (Guildhall Library & Greater London Archives Network 3rd ed. 1994)

Society of Genealogists publications: various subjects

Sir Anthony Wagner, *English Genealogy* (Phillimore 1983)

J. B. Whitmore, *A Genealogical Guide* (Walford 1953)

GENETICS
Steve Jones, *The Language of Genes* (HarperCollins 1993)

——, *In The Blood* (HarperCollins 1996)

SURNAMES
Patricia Hanks and Flavia Hodges, *A Dictionary of Surnames* (OUP 1988)

R. A. McKinley, *A History of British Surnames* (Longman 1990)

—— (ed.), *English Surnames Series* (1973–96)

P. H. Reaney and R. M. Wilson, *A Dictionary of English Surnames* (3rd ed., OUP 1995)

PALAEOGRAPHY
Eileen Gooder, *Latin for Local History* (Longmans 1978)

L. C. Hector, *The Handwriting of English Documents* (Arnold 1979)

R. E. Latham, *Revised Medieval Latin Word-List* (British Academy/ OUP 1965)

C. T. Martin, *The Record Interpreter* (Kohler and Coombes 1982)

CENSUS

J. Gibson and E. Hampson, *Marriage, Census and Other Indexes for Family Historians* (FFHS 1998)

Edward Higgs, *Making Sense of the Census* (PRO 1989)

——, *A Clearer Sense of the Census* (PRO 1996)

Susan Lumas, *Making Use of the Census* (PRO 2nd ed. 1997)

NONCONFORMIST, CATHOLIC AND JEWISH RECORDS

N. Currer-Briggs, R. Gambier, *Huguenot Ancestry* (Phillimore 1985)

Michael Gandy, *Catholic Parishes in England, Wales and Scotland* (an atlas) (1993)

——, *Catholic Missions and Registers (1700–1880)* (1993)

My Ancestors Were . . . series (Society of Genealogists)

David Shorney, *Protestant Nonconformity and Roman Catholicism: A guide to sources in the PRO* (PRO 1996)

D. J. Steel, *National Index of Parish Registers Vol II, Sources for Nonconformist Genealogy and Family History* (Society of Genealogists 1973)

D. J. Steel and E. R. Samuel, *The National Index of Parish Registers Vol. III, Sources for Roman Catholic and Jewish Genealogy and Family History* (Society of Genealogists 1974)

WILLS

J. Gibson, *Probate Jurisdictions: Where to Look for Wills* (FFHS 1994)

Miriam Scott, *Prerogative Court of Canterbury Wills and Other Probate Records* (PRO 1997)

LAND AND TAX RECORDS

N. W. Alcock, *Old Title Deeds* (Phillimore 1986)

M. Ellis, *Using Manorial Records* (PRO 1994)

P. D. A. Harvey, *Manorial Records* (British Record Association 1984)

M. Jurkowski, C. Smith and D. Crook, *Lay Taxes in England and Wales 1188–1688* (PRO 1998)

Manorial Documents Register: at Quality House, London (see address list). Website: http://www.hmc.gov.uk/main.htm

SERVICES
S. Fowler, P. Elliott, R. C. Nesbit, C. Goulter, *RAF Records in the PRO* (PRO 1994)

S. Fowler, W. Spencer *Army Records for Family Historians* (PRO 1998)

S. Fowler, W. Spencer, S. Tamblin, *Army Service Records of the First World War* (PRO 1998)

Gerald Hamilton-Edwards, *In Search of Army Ancestry* (Phillimore 1977)

Norman Holding, *World War One Army Ancestry* (FFHS 1982)

——, *More Sources of World War One Army Ancestry* (FFHS 1991)

N. A. M. Rodger, *Naval Records for Genealogists* (PRO 1988)

K. Smith, C. Watts, M. Watts, *Records of Merchant Shipping & Seamen* (PRO 1998)

Garth Thomas, *Records of the Royal Marines* (PRO)

Eunice Wilson, *The Records of the Royal Air Force* (FFHS 1991)

SCOTLAND, WALES AND IRELAND
Kathleen B. Cory, *Tracing Your Scottish Ancestry* (Polygon 1990)

Gerald Hamilton-Edwards, *In Search of Scottish Ancestry* (Phillimore 1988)

C. Sinclair, *Tracing your Scottish Ancestors: A Guide to Ancestry Research in the Scottish Record Office* (HMSO 1990)

Gerald Hamilton-Edwards, *In Search of Welsh Ancestry* (Phillimore 1986)

J. Istance, E. E. Cann, *Researching Family History in Wales* (FFHS 1996)

J. and S. Rowlands, *Welsh Family History: A Guide to Research* (FFHS 2nd ed. 1998)

J. Grenham, *Tracing Your Irish Ancestors* (Gill & Macmillan 1992)

Ian Maxwell, *Tracing Your Ancestors in Northern Ireland* (PRONI 1997)

EMIGRATION

Noel Currer-Briggs, *Worldwide Family History* (Routledge & Kegan Paul 1982)

Anne Bromell, *Tracing Family History in New Zealand* (GP Books, Wellington 1988)

P. William Filby, *et al* (eds.), *Passenger and Immigration Lists Index* and *Passenger and Immigration Lists Bibliography 1538–1900* (Detroit: 1980–98)

Guy Grannum, *Tracing your West Indian Ancestors* (PRO 1995)

Guildhall Library, *The British Overseas: a guide to records of their births, baptisms, marriages, deaths and burials available in the United Kingdom* (Guildhall Library, 3rd (revised) ed. 1995)

Nick Vine Hall, *Tracing Your Family History in Australia* (Rigby, Adelaide 1985)

HERALDRY

Thomas Woodcock, *The Oxford Guide to Heraldry* (OUP 1988)

David Williamson, *Debrett's Guide to Heraldry and Regalia* (Headline 1992)

MAPS

William Foot, *Maps for Family History: A guide to the records of the Tithe, Valuation Office, and National Farm Surveys of England and Wales, 1836–1943* (PRO 1994)

Cecil Humphery-Smith (ed.), *The Phillimore Atlas and Index of Parish Registers* (Phillimore 1995)

ACKNOWLEDGEMENTS

It is impossible for a single author to do justice to a subject as complex as genealogy. We have, therefore, been fortunate in being able to assemble contributions from many specialists, but I must especially thank my colleague, Royston Gambier for his invaluable help in the compilation of this book. His experience both as a practising genealogist and as a teacher, as well as a former chairman and co-founder of the Federation of Family History Societies is of a very special character. Without his assistance and critical attention to detail it would not have been possible to produce this book in the time at our disposal. I am likewise indebted to Hugh Peskett and Charles Teviot for their valuable contributions on Celtic ancestry and on the records of the services and professions. I must also acknowledge my special gratitude to Peter de V. B. Dewar FSA (Scot) for his valuable assistance in preparing the chapter on heraldry and to Jane Paterson for her contribution on handwriting.

Among the many whom I consulted by letter and through their published works I must thank in particular Margaret Audin, Count Camajani, Professor Hans Eysenck, Sebastian de Ferranti, Francis

Leeson, Isobel Mordy, Hugh Montgomery-Massingberd and Edgar Samuel.

I am grateful to Susan Morris and Juliet Burgess of Debrett Ancestry Research who have thoroughly revised and updated the original book, and to Anne-Marie Ehrlich for her indefatigable help with the illustrations.

PUBLISHER'S NOTE

The following exceptions exist to the copyright information listed on page iv.

Copyright © 1979 Noel Currer-Briggs and Royston Gambier: Appendix I.

Copyright © 1981 Hugh Peskett: Chapter 5, sections on marriage licences; Chapter 8, Dating; Chapter 9; Chapter 10, section on Jewish Ancestry; Chapter 14, section on Australia and New Zealand.

Copyright © 1981 Jane Paterson: Chapter 2, section on Handwriting.

Copyright © 1989 Noel Currer-Briggs: Chapter 14, sections on USA, Canada and South Africa; Chapter 17.

PICTURE CREDITS

The authors and publishers would like to thank the following for supplying illustrations on illustration page numbers: 6, 7, 8 Amsterdams Historisch Museum; 2 Lady Soames (Her Majesty's Stationery Office); 10, 11, 14, 15, 16 The Public Record Office; 4, 9, 12 The Society of Genealogists.

INDEX

residence, records of 46–7; *see also* addresses

Robinson, John Martin 125

Rodger, N.A.M. 101

Roman Catholic Church *see* Catholic records

Roman civilization and society 5–7, 10, 23–4

Roman Law 76

Roots 2, 9

Rose, Sir George 58

Rosenthal, Erich 8

Roth, Cecil 85

Royal Air Force 47, 105, 149

Royal Artillery 102

Royal Colleges of Physicians and Surgeons 108–9

Royal Commission on Historical Manuscripts 94, 149

Royal Flying Corps 105

royal genealogies 10

Royal Geographical Society 131

Royal Irish Academy 78

Royal Marines 101

Royal Naval Biography 100

St Helens 130

St Petersburg, register of the Independent Church of 60

samplers 35

'Sasines' 76

Saxton, Christopher 128

Scotland 27, 37–8, 63, 70, 73–6, 88, 124–5, 147, 161–2

Scottish Record Office 76, 163

script, different styles of 17

seamen's tickets 105

Secretary Hand 17, 21

'Seigneur', title of 125–6

service records 34, 47, 99–106

'Services of Heirs' 76

Sextons' Books 67

ships' records 101

Shorney, David 61

snobbery 2, 11

Society of Apothecaries 108–9

Society of Friends

Library of 149

see also Quakers

Society of Genealogists 1–2, 11, 38, 43, 59, 61, 110, 127, 149

Soho 83

solicitors 109

South Africa 120–21

Southport records centre 43, 49, 149

Spain 126

Speed, John 128

Speenhamland System 65

spelling of surnames 26

Spitalfields 83

Spufford, Peter 127

Stamp Act 58

Steel, D.J. 61

still-births 47

Stuart, Margaret 37

Sudbury, Baron 126

Suetonius Tranquillus 16

surnames 23–36

essential characteristic of 26

five types 27

historical development of 24–7

multiple 28

North American 28–9

research on 36

unusual, societies for 3

Swinnerton, Sir Iain 32–3; *see also Foreword*

Synod of Rheims 25

Tacitus 25

taping of conversations 36